THE
MARTYN LEWIS
INTERVIEWS
Volume One

THE

MARTYN LEWIS

INTERVIEWS

Volume One

Famous achievers talk frankly to
Martyn Lewis about their route to the top

First published in 1997

© Martyn Lewis

Martyn Lewis has asserted his right
under the Copyright, Designs and
Patent Act 1988 to be identified as
the author of this work

ISBN 1 85291 135 2

First published
in Great Britain in 1997 by
Lennard Publishing
A division of Lennard Associates
Mackerye End, Harpenden
Herts AL5 5DR

Printed and bound in Great Britain by
Clays Ltd, St Ives plc

CONTENTS

Foreword   6

1.   Jackie Stewart   9

2.   Sir George Martin   27

3.   Anita Roddick   55

4.   Bruce Oldfield   75

5.   Lord Saatchi   101

6.   Andrew Neil   123

7.   François Pienaar   149

FOREWORD

It is clear that for some the desire to achieve success is the driving force in their lives. Others envy those who have acquired it. However success is achieved, it usually generates widespread media attention and private interest – all the more so because there seems to be no set formula to being successful, no real universal standard for measuring it, and no guarantee that it will be sustained.

I talk to people from all walks of life who (with varying degrees of public prominence) are generally considered to be successful in their particular field. I ask how they have achieved their success: what mistakes, setbacks and failures marked their progress; how they overcame them; how they view the remaining challenges ahead; and the advice and guidance they now give to people entering their chosen profession.

Throughout there are inevitably powerful comments on the 'success ethic'. What are the forces operating against success, trying to pull the successful down? Why is success often despised in Britain, while the USA puts it on a pedestal? What are the visible consequences of those differing attitudes? These are all questions explored throughout the book, but the key factor is that people talk about success in their own terms – no editorial spin is put on their comments – their judgements and opinions are recorded unvarnished, allowing the reader to judge.

We in the media quite properly spend much time in news and current affairs looking at how and why things go wrong. But we make the mistake of giving too little space to things going right! A book rich in different definitions of success goes some way towards redressing the balance – and should be instantly attractive to the huge number of people throughout the country who support the call I made three years ago for the media to adopt a more balanced news agenda.

Martyn Lewis
April 1997

'It is not the critic who counts: not the man who points out how the strong man stumbles, or where the doer of deeds could have done them better. The credit belongs to the man who is actually in the arena, whose face is marred by dust and sweat and blood: who strives valiantly; who errs, and comes short again and again, because there is no effort without error and shortcoming; but who does actually strive to do the deeds; who knows the great enthusiasms, the great devotions; who spends himself in a worthy cause; who at the best knows in the end the triumph of high achievement, and who at the worst, if he fails, at least fails while daring greatly, so that his place shall never be with those cold and timid souls who know neither victory nor defeat.'
Theodore Rooseveldt, address at the Sorbonne, Paris, France,
23 April 1910.

'As life is action and passion, it is required of a man that he should share the action of his time at peril of being judged not to have lived.'
Oliver Wendell Holmes

JACKIE STEWART

Three times Formula One World Motor Racing Champion, Jackie Stewart left school at 15 as 'a complete disaster'. Undiagnosed dyslexia had given him 'a humiliating time' – with pupils and teachers labelling him 'stupid, dumb and thick' because he couldn't read or recite the alphabet. At 58, that basic classroom mantra still eludes him, but his life is a formidable example of how an unpromising start is no real guide to a person's potential. 'Real success,' he says, 'is reaching your true potential – at whatever level that might be.'

When he retired from motor racing at the age of 34, he was a multi-millionaire with a mansion in Switzerland, and a jet-setting life-style which continued as a chain of major international companies including Ford, Rolex and Moet and Chandon sought his advice and his name. He also returned to an early love, setting up the Jackie Stewart shooting school at Gleneagles Hotel.

Then, 20 years later, he was back in Formula One, this time running (along with his son, Paul) the brand new Stewart Grand Prix team, backed by Ford. He never stops.

His 'get-up-and-go' and meticulous attention to detail often exhaust those around him. Despite his dyslexia, he has taught himself to become an inspirational and hugely motivating public speaker. Most successful people, he believes, 'have difficulty managing the money and the power they suddenly acquire.' His solution is mind-management – the need to remove emotion from your business life because 'the heart is the most dangerous thing. Never,' he insists, 'allow the intoxication of the moment to take hold.' He believes that bad luck is created through lack of preparation – and draws on his own experience to offer advice on tackling life's inevitable setbacks.

Jackie Stewart, what is your definition of success?

Success could be recognized as the achievement of any individual's full potential. A remarkable number of people get some lesser form of success without doing that, but real success is reaching your true potential, whatever God's gift to you was. Someone who can't read or write may be successful in reaching a level of achievement that would be much easier for someone else, but for that person their success is in reaching the ultimate limit within their capability.

How important a factor is recognition?

I don't think other people's recognition is very important as long as the person himself knows that he could not have done a better job. There are many times when I may not have won a race, but I did a good job and achieved as much as I could ever have done on that particular day. It is very egotistical to want public recognition of your success; that's not important because it's other people's perception of your achievement or failure and this may sometimes be accurate, but is more often inaccurate.

So the essential judgement is to be true to yourself and to make a decision about whether you have succeeded inside yourself and not be swayed by what people outside might be saying about you?

Absolutely. My father used to always say, 'See yourself as others see you,' but in this case it might be more appropriate to say, 'You can kid a lot of people but you can't kid yourself.' You have to be bluntly honest with yourself in your own evaluation. But when I was younger and first won something, the recognition of that success was something that gave me great personal satisfaction because it was my first experience of being given credit for achieving anything.

Do you remember when that was?

That was when I was about 14 or 15, and I won my first clay pigeon shooting event. I became quite good at shooting, but I was dyslexic – and still am – and when you're at school and you can't read a simple passage from a book, you're abused by the sniggers and the coughing of your peers drawing attention to your inability. Such humiliation has a deep effect on a young person, so if you are at last recognized as being good at something, that means a great deal more to you than it would have done to anybody else. Suddenly to get praise instead of abuse is very rewarding, but you've got to be very careful that that isn't intoxicating. People get intoxicated by their supposed success in every line of work, and I think it's terribly important to be able to see what your faults are. If you are really honest, your own criticism of your performance will be more focused than any other person's observations, and more useful in helping you to deliver at a higher level.

I may have won some races or, in business, I may have achieved some deals that I know I worked really hard on, but there are other occasions when I am aware that I didn't do a particularly good job, and I still achieved what others perceived as success.

To me, John McEnroe is a good example. John McEnroe had poor mind management, but incredible natural talent. The annoyance and the anger that he displayed so unattractively was in most cases aimed at himself; it was the frustration of not having played a shot as he had intended, giving the advantage to his opponent. His inability to achieve what he wanted to do frustrated him so much that if something else happened, a bad line call or something of that kind, he couldn't control that frustration any more. In a competitive world if you make mistakes you allow other people to gain the advantage.

But how do you control that frustration?

Mind management. I think the most important thing that I learned, both from my shooting and my motor racing, to prepare me for the business world, was to remove emotion; the heart is the most dangerous thing, you must never allow emotion to take hold.

But can you ever completely remove emotion? We are human beings after all.

Yes, but I think the really good performers clinically attack their performance to remove the little flaws that may not be obvious to the observer, to the critic, to the aficionado even. The right choice of words is important to a politician or in a business negotiation, and there is always room for improvement.

On the race track someone like Frankie Dettori will have made mistakes and yet won races, but he knows he's made the mistake even though nobody else noticed. But he was able to get away with it because the really good performers can succeed even on their off-days.

Never allow the intoxication of the moment to take hold, you may have just broken the lap record but you haven't finished the race, you may have taken the meeting through to a 'yes, in principle', and 'subject to contract', but if you don't see things through in a level-headed way the chances are the race will be lost or the deal will fall apart.

Again, during business negotiations somebody might annoy you to a point where you get angry and, if you don't control your emotions in a very clinical fashion, you'll respond angrily. How many times have you said things in anger that later you regretted? In family situations, in human relationships, in many circumstances you can suddenly become so vulnerable to your own lack of control that a situation becomes irretrievable, your spontaneous response can destroy the deal, destroy the relationship, sometimes for ever.

In motor racing, if you get annoyed at making a mistake and letting someone pass you, or if you get angry at another driver's aggressive behaviour, you'll probably drive off the road, so what's the point? As they say, 'Don't get mad get even,' but you've got to have mind management not to get mad and you've got to position yourself strategically to get even or take advantage.

You talked earlier about your dyslexia – what was it like for you at school to be labelled as you were an under-achiever, a no-hoper?

You were labelled stupid, dumb and thick because you couldn't read or recite the alphabet. Even today, if you gave me £10 million, I couldn't run through the alphabet. I don't know the words of the Lord's Prayer and I don't know the words of my own National Anthem although I've stood while it has been played at many victory ceremonies. The wiring system is not right up there: it's not a man-made problem in the sense that I didn't concentrate or pay attention at school, it's just something that occurs to some extent in one in ten young people, and more in boys than girls. The humiliation, the mental abuse, the lack of self-esteem that you experience leave their mark forever, more so in those days because dyslexia wasn't properly recognized by the teachers.

I left school at 15 as a complete disaster, to the great relief of the school as well as myself; but more to the relief of myself, because it was a daily abuse, it was like somebody hitting you on the same spot everyday. When that happens the bruise gets bigger and the pain gets deeper. There are so many young people still in that position today; they've got inferiority complexes, they're shy, they'll never look you in the eye, they'll avoid situations, they can't fill in a form. I couldn't fill in my driving test form and I still can't fill in any forms, I need secretaries to do that sort of thing for me. But I'm lucky, God gave me hands, eyes and co-ordination that allowed me first of all to shoot, which gave me back some self-respect and then to drive racing cars which brought new confidence.

On the other hand I don't know anything about the history of my country; I know my geography because I've been to places, and I can look at a map of the world and identify where I've been, but I still don't have a great knowledge of the English language. The language that I understand today has been learned from conversation rather than from reading.

In talking about my shooting school or a feasibility study that I'm doing for a new shooting school, I'll mention 'topography'. Topography is a word I picked up in someone else's conversation and I asked what it meant. I liked the sound of the word and now I use it myself. The other day my mobile phone wasn't working very well and they told me it was because of 'topospherics', now I will remember topospherics, that's a big one for me!

I do a lot of public speaking today, much of it in my work for Ford, but I always assume that the audience is as dumb as I am. I go to great lengths to paint as colourful, as pretty a picture of what I'm trying to illustrate in words so that they will better understand, and I take longer to explain this than most other people. I have to be sure in my mind that they understand what I'm saying because I've suffered so much myself from not understanding the question or the instructions.

Even today I went to the wrong room to meet you for this interview; because I'm a dyslexic, numbers just don't mean anything to me and I got the hotel room number wrong. I have a busy schedule today and I spent 12 minutes, I took note how long it took me, to sort things out. So here I am late and frustrated because of my own inability; you never get over it, you only learn how to get round it, but on the positive side it has made me try harder.

I was going to ask you, are you more ambitious because you had to fight your way out of this desperately difficult start in life?

Because I'm fairly independent I'm not so worried about other people any longer, but to this day I still have something to prove to myself. I lost a deal the other day and I rescued it this morning at 6.00 a.m. because I can't give up, I don't want to give up, I've failed if I give up.

So the potential for success can come for two reasons – it can come through encouragement, through having a strong mentor or someone backing you or it can come, as in your case, through having immense disadvantage and something within yourself saying, 'I've got to fight to overcome this.' That's where ambition is born?

I think that's stronger than having a mentor behind you. You can ask other people for advice, you can go to some business guru and ask him what he would have done in similar circumstances, but then to some extent you're doing his deal.

You've got to find your own way of achieving the success that you're after. It is important to be ambitious at whatever you want to do, and then you've got to find out how that can best be accomplished, often it takes a long time to find out.

Here I am at 57 years of age and still learning. Perhaps my strongest asset is my attention to detail. I say I'm the president of the menial task division; I need things to be clean, I need things to be tidy. In my office or even in this hotel, I'll always pick up a piece of paper that's lying on the floor. Now if I do that my staff will see that they should do it. If they don't, if they pass it and I pick it up they realize their mistake. The best way to help people understand what is important and what's not important is by example. If you look after the details, the chances are the bigger things will fall into place because it's all the little things that make up the big picture.

You might think that, because of its size or bureaucracy, the Ford motor company's a giant, but Jac Nasser, who is now president of the company, doesn't think of it as a big company he thinks of it as a conglomeration of small companies and he's right.

A body doesn't die because the body as a whole has decayed; you discover there's an organ – a liver, a kidney, a heart, a brain – that's gone wrong, and if that organ is repaired and kept in good working order the chances are the body will function quite well.

How big a part do you think luck plays in success? Going right back to your early days, was it luck that took you into motor racing in the first place and was it luck that kept you on top?

I don't believe in bad luck, I believe in good luck. I believe that bad luck is created through lack of preparation, through lack of skills or talents, or poor judgement of people. If a young man gets into crime, it's not bad luck, he's chosen to mix with the wrong people and should have seen the dangers ahead.

Another of my father's sayings was, 'If you fly with the crows, you are liable to be shot at'; if you go with the wrong group that's not bad luck, that's bad judgement. If I had been in a racing car that was badly prepared I probably wouldn't have won many races. It wasn't good luck that I chose the right teams to drive for, the right engineers, the right team manager, the right tyre man, engine man, suspension man, gear-box man. So it's not bad luck that the car breaks down at every race; there's a very good reason for it, either somebody hasn't tightened something up or the part was not good enough in the first place, designed poorly or manufactured badly. Good luck in most cases comes through the misfortune of others.

At the expense of others?

Yes, the poor performance of others in some cases. I have been lucky on occasions but usually it's been bad luck for someone else.

When I retired from racing I gave most of my trophies away because I thought having them in a big room, all glittering and shining, was very self-serving: 'Look who I am and how clever I've been.' I didn't like it so I gave most of them away to people who'd helped me in my career. I've kept several. I kept the Princess Grace trophy from Monaco, I kept the American Grand Prix because it was a lovely punch bowl, and of my four wins in the Spanish Grand Prix I kept one in particular because, in that race, I came from sixth position and I won the race without ever passing a car, they all broke down or crashed. This was the perfect example of why you should never give up. I drove as well as I could on that day, but because of either my car, my tyres, myself or whatever, I was never going to finish better than sixth. I kept that trophy, and I have it in my office, as a reminder that you should never think that just because things aren't quite right you can't achieve something.

You can still win through determination, through staying there. If you don't stay there trying your best, you're never going to do it; so you've got to stick with it, you've got to persevere, you've got to work at it. It's not just a case of saying, 'I'm not going to win so, hey, who cares?' You should never, ever give up.

How much of success is down to the individual and how much is down to the team behind that individual in motor racing?

Enormous dependency on the team, you've got to have the best car, the best chassis with the best engine and the best people.

Damon Hill won the 1996 world championship but, not taking anything from Damon, the Williams car and that team gave him the world championship, no doubt in my mind at all.

Schumacher was the best driver of 1996, he is the best driver in the world at the present time, but his car wasn't good enough, the team wasn't good enough, the package wasn't good enough. Now Ferrari have got the most expensive driver, the most expensive team manager, the most expensive designer, the most expensive test facility and the most expensive factory with the largest budget and they haven't won a world championship for 17 years. Something is wrong.

Williams are not short of money after all they've achieved, so they've got good sponsors and good budgets too, but Frank Williams, Patrick Head and Adrian Newey, who is an aerodynamicist as well as a designer, created the best engineered Grand Prix car in the world, and I think at least four drivers could have won the world championship with that car, maybe six.

So you definitely need the right people, not just a good driver. Equally if you've put all of that money into a team, you've got to have as good a driver as you can buy to match the skills of the other people.

Have you ever felt like giving up? Have you ever felt like saying 'Right, I've done it all, that's it, I could happily coast through the rest of my life'?

Why would you want to give up? What is there to give up? My wife would like to spend more time with me, we would like to take longer holidays and have a more relaxed life, but I can't do that. I'm committed to several contracts that I went into with my eyes open, that I have to honour, and in any case I enjoy and get fulfillment from my work. I feel I've been put on this earth to do whatever I should do, and the things that I'm driven to doing I want to do well.

Are you a driven person?

Yes, very driven.

And from what you're saying there has been an element of sacrifice in your personal life. Do you think that every successful person has to sacrifice a slice of their personal life?

Americans say there are no free lunches, you don't get the very best in life without paying for it in some form. We have been married for 34 years, so it hasn't been such a sacrifice that it's had a negative effect on our family life.

We have two very healthy sons who are well adjusted boys; they've been brought up well by their mother and I hope in some way by myself, and given a good example of how to behave in life.

From the 60s through to the 90s we haven't had the problems that have affected so many young people and their mother has had a great deal to do with that. Helen and I are still here, happy and together, despite a turbulent lifestyle and, for a while, the glamour and excitement of the Grand Prix circuit. But she didn't marry a racing driver, I was a clay pigeon shooter then and we've moved from one sphere to another to another.

We're fairly well adjusted, we haven't allowed ourselves to become intoxicated either by the lifestyle or any of the benefits or privileges that lifstyle brings. It's very important not to get carried away by this so-called success.

Many people have difficulty managing the money and

power that they suddenly acquire. You see some extraordinarily arrogant people who have had only a small degree of success, but the most successful people, the really big players, are the easiest in the world to deal with.

Do you think that everyone who is successful has to have experienced some form of sacrifice or failure at some stage in their lives?

Yes I think you've got to establish your values. Nobody is going to acquire wisdom and maturity at an early age; first of all, as a young person, you gain experience and from the experience you gain knowledge and from the knowledge you sometimes get wisdom and maybe one day you get maturity.

When you first earn a lot of money and you can afford things you could never have had before, it's very pleasant; you sometimes get quite a high from it and you can easily become quite arrogant in the eyes of someone else who is less fortunate. You have to learn how to deal with it. You can't do that overnight.

So when you achieve sudden, fast success, how do you keep your feet on the ground, what formula would you offer?

I think one of the advantages that I have had is that, as I have gone along, the people I have become acquainted with and with whom I have had any sort of relationship have, almost exclusively, been more successful than me; they've either got a lot more money, a higher position, or more influence and power.

It's easier for me to keep my feet on the ground in their company than if I had a bunch of court jesters around me, sycophants making me feel good, look good, pumping me up; I hate that. You're in danger of not seeing life as it really is, and then when you get into other company where you are not so big, you don't know how to handle it.

I think it's a good lesson to always try and associate with people whom you respect and admire.

Let me take you back to the year when you spun off the track in the Belgian Grand Prix. You were trapped, you were soaked in petrol, you had a broken shoulder, a cracked rib. Some people might have said, 'That's enough, I'm out,' and yet you were back driving two months later. What was it inside you that made you want to get back on the track after an experience like that?

It's part of the business: it's what everybody else did; it was part of the culture; it was part of the procedure; it was what was expected of you.

The first time I got back in a car again my knees trembled on the peddles, but that's something that you overcome and again that's mind management. You say, 'Listen you've done this all your professional life, there's nothing to stop you doing it again. Come on let's get the act together.'

Racing team managers sometimes recognize that. I had a an accident in South Africa in 1973, in qualifying; it was a big one, at 176 m.p.h., it was a brake problem. It could have easily got to me, so as soon as I got back to the pits Ken Tyrrell immediately brought my team-mate in, put me into his car and told me to go out and re-qualify.

It was the correct decision, you've got to get over that sort of experience quickly and recalibrate your mind. Again it's mind management, and if it bothers you too much then you're in the wrong business, then it is time to stop.

What do you think are the most important qualities you need to be successful?

For me attention to detail, mind management and trying constantly to have respect for other people.

And what would you say are the biggest enemies of success?

Ego, or self-adulation, over-confidence and hiding from reality.

Who are the people you regard as being highly successful? Who are the people you admire past or present?

His Majesty King Hussein of Jordan, because he's a real man, he has lived his life his way, he has done it in the face of considerable adversity. He's had something like 27 attempts on his life which he deals with very diligently but respectfully; he has achieved tremendous amounts for other people and done it in a responsible fashion and with dignity. He's a man whom women like as a man because he's a gentle man. I've never known a man with better manners, and yet so powerful in his own way; he has been personally responsible for so much of the re-shaping of the Middle East.

As a businessman Lord King re-shaped an enormous bureaucratic nightmare in transforming British Airways into the world's favourite airline and a world leader.

He's now a man of mature years with tremendous experience, a man of knowledge and dignity who came from modest beginnings and carries whatever he has been given, be it knighthood or peerage, with the same dignity.

There are so many people I admire, people like Agnelli who has been able to shape a nation to some extent through the number of companies on which he has had an influence – banks, media, car makers, property. On a global basis he is a very major player.

Then there's Roger Hill, the mechanic who brought me three world championships. Roger Hill was probably better at what he did than I ever was at what I did, so he was a real achiever and reached far beyond his own expectations, beyond his own perception of his ability. I also admire Ken

Tyrrell, he's over 70 years of age, he's still going on, his team isn't as successful today as it once was, but Ken's always kept his own principles, his own morals, his own commitments and his own integrity. There's a whole lot of people.

Is there a downside to success?

Not that I'm aware of. You lose some of the privacy that you may wish in life but, in my opinion, the privileges that you gain are far beyond those that you lose. If privacy is a concern it's usually because someone doesn't know how to deal with the situation and allows the problem to get out of proportion, to become exaggerated.

In pursuit of success have you ever done anything you wished you hadn't done?

There were times I might have behaved differently. But if I had my life to run again, I wouldn't change a lot.

Part and parcel of success is criticism of one kind or another. How do you weather criticism? Is there a formula for doing that?

I think you've got to take some notice of it because it's somebody else's perception of your performance or your behaviour; you would be wrong to ignore it.

Objective criticism is very healthy and you've got to think about it but sometimes you've got to say, 'Listen, I can't do anything about it so let it go.'

You have had a very successful career, there is no need for you to work anymore, and yet you are taking on the most difficult challenge in motor racing, which is starting your own team from scratch. Why go through all that hassle?

I really don't have an easy answer to it, but it doesn't occur to me that what anybody has done in the past has got anything at all to do with what one should do now or in the future. Business opportunities arrive, or crop up from time to time and one never really thinks about the downside, even though it may be there. My life has always been built on the basis that nothing is going to be easy – it's just a question of trying to reduce the downside elements: be it risk, discomfort or hassle.

I would not have done this at all had I not already had a son and a business in existence – which is what I had in Paul Stewart Racing. That business had to go somewhere to develop any further and this is the evolution of that. If we were going to go into motor racing in the big time, then Formula One was where we had to be. The combination of Paul's ambitions and the sudden possibility of Ford Motor Company being able to provide us with exclusive use of their Formula One factory engine for five years, was an opportunity that would probably not have come along again for a very long time.

What advice would you give to young people who want to succeed as you have succeeded?

To give total commitment to whatever they choose to do. There's no half way mark, you just can't work at a level of mediocrity; it's got to be a total commitment, it's got to be an absolute focus, an absolute driven desire to succeed or achieve. Attention to detail is probably one thing I major on above all else. Try to eliminate all of the interruptions that may stop the success or achievement that you are aiming for. You have got to be on the ball all the time: to be pro-active; to be thinking ahead; to be looking at the potential downside risks, and if you don't address them, see them in reality, and try to plan around them. Above all you have to have integrity; without integrity you have nothing. It's no good trying to work a fast one, you get back what you put in and people who go for the short-cut, the cheap fix, will never make it long-term. They may make money, but they'll always be vulnerable, they will be found out, and they will lose in the end.

And what would you like people to say about you when your time comes to leave this planet?

That I had integrity.

SIR GEORGE MARTIN

The man who discovered the Beatles and became one of the greatest record producers in the world had to give up piano lessons as a child because his parents couldn't afford them.

Just after his 17th birthday, with World War Two well under way, signed up for the Fleet Air Arm, learning 'all sorts of new disciplines'. When demobbed, he used his ex-serviceman's grant for three years' study at the Guildhall School of Music – after which he settled for a job in the BBC music library, because it gave him 'the freedom to compose and play his own songs in the evenings'.

Then, out of the blue, came an offer of a job with Parlophone EMI, where he produced virtually everything from Mozart to jazz – and even Enid Blyton's Noddy stories! His rise was meteoric. At 29, he became Head of Parlophone – no one that young had ever been in charge of a record label before – and worked with artists such as Peter Sellers, Spike Milligan, Charlie Drake, Michael Flanders and Donald Swan.

It was envy of the success being enjoyed by his friend Norrie Paramour with the newly discovered Cliff Richard that drove him to take a chance with the Beatles when every other record company in London had turned them down. With other singers like Cilla Black and Freddie and the Dreamers on his label, 1963 saw records he had produced hold the number one slot in the hit parade for no fewer than 39 weeks. When EMI rejected his attempts to obtain a share of royalties for producers, he left to form his own company, Associated Independent Recordings (AIR) – still his pride and joy. The Beatles went with him, and he never looked back. He rolled into his 70th year as active as ever.

Sir George, what is your definition of success?

I think success is probably achieving what you want to achieve, without hurting anyone in the process. You go through life trying to do what you can, as best you can. And if you strike success, you get applauded, and if you hit failure you get all the downside. If you're lucky you have more of the success than the failure.

So it's not a good idea to say, 'I want to be successful,' without having a very clear idea of the area of life that you wish to be successful in?

I suppose every young person has the ambition to be successful, and that, in most young people's eyes, means being rich and famous. They don't realize this isn't all that it might appear; of course it's better to have more money than less, and of course it's nice to be wooed by people and flattering that people recognize you. But I think true success is getting to a position where you are at peace with yourself, where you know that whatever you have done has been good for other people. Success for me also means a successful family, having the people around me that I love and having that love returned.

Is there not an inevitable conflict though, between someone pursuing a successful career and someone who wants to have a successful family life? How do you get the balance right between the two?

It's very difficult and the first time round I didn't. My first marriage ended in failure. I got married too young; I was engaged when I was 19 and in those days I was a very ambitious young musician. When I started at Abbey Road I was seduced by the business of recording. It was a fascinating business, and I loved it. I worked extraordinarily long hours and that, obviously, had some effect upon the marriage. It wasn't the only reason the marriage failed, but it was a contributing factor.

When I married again, I married a lady who had been in the business and understood it, and she had all the tolerance that was necessary to cope with the extraordinary hours that I would keep. With the Beatles, we would work right through the night and into the following morning, but she understood this and supported it, and without her I would not have been successful.

So it is true that behind every successful person there is a partner who is providing all the support and back-up that you need?

In my case, it's been absolutely essential. I can't contemplate life without my wife, and those people who are loners, who don't have that benefit, that blessedness of having a good woman, I think they make it more difficult for themselves, and I think they become inward-looking. I think they have to be if they don't have someone to respond to. Having a partner teaches you to look outside yourself.

To what extent is success a product of your background and your upbringing, going right back to the early days?

Well, I suppose it was imbued in me by my parents, because they weren't very well off, but they were good people and both were very hard-working. My father was a carpenter and my mother came from a rather better family than my father, but being poor she had to work awfully hard. She herself was quite talented and always wanted her son to do his very best and urged me on at school. I went to a state elementary school to begin with, and then I got a scholarship to a Jesuit college, St Ignatius in North London, but I didn't go to university because the war was on, and I left school when I was 16. But by this time I was running a dance band, which again I was encouraged to do because my parents thought the music was lovely, although they weren't musicians. There was no music in the family but I just had this natural talent.

So the interest in music was there right from the start?

Well, it was a curious thing. We always had a piano in our household; I can't remember the house not having a piano. My sister, who was three years older than I, was first taught by an aunt and then had lessons for two years, but we couldn't afford lessons for two children, so I missed out. But I would imitate what my sister did and I really cannot remember not being able to play tunes on the piano. I was playing on the piano when I was four or five, making up little pieces.

Right from those early days, did you sense that music was going to be a potential career for you?

No, I didn't. I just ran a band and earned some money – it was a lovely hobby. And my parents never considered music because it was like the acting profession; it might be fun to do amateur dramatics, but my goodness, it wasn't a career for a decent gentleman.

My mother said, 'Do something really solid, take up a profession. You're good at maths, you're good at drawing, architecture sounds a good idea.' My father went along with that, and I was certainly very interested in design. In fact, what I wanted to do most of all when I was in my teens was to be an aircraft designer.

And was that why, when you left school, you went into the Fleet Air Arm as an observer?

When I knew I had to go into one of the Services, I knew I didn't want to go into the Army, but I loved flying and I loved boats too, so the Fleet Air Arm was a natural choice. I signed up when I was 17; I didn't tell my mother and she was absolutely shaken, poor woman, when I went home and told her. 'Oh my God,' she said, 'you're going to get killed.' Well I wasn't, thank the Lord.

What did that time, in the Armed Services, actually do for you? Did it change you in any way?

Absolutely. It changed me beyond belief. I'd been very much a mother's boy and the darling of the family, so to speak, and I was probably spoiled, but when I joined the Fleet Air Arm I didn't see my family for nearly two years.

I was sent abroad, I'd done my training and I started flying – first in Swordfish and then, in our operational squadron, in Barracudas. In that transition you had to learn all sorts of disciplines, which I hadn't had before, and you became an officer. I went to Greenwich and learned a different way of life in the Wardroom there; I came home a man. I left as a boy and my mother didn't recognize this fellow in the Sub-Lieutenant's uniform.

When you came out of the Fleet Air Arm you went to the Guildhall School of Music, by that time the ambition to develop music was firmly set within you?

Well I had a kind of fairy godfather in the shape of a piano professor called Sidney Harrison, and I'd corresponded with him all through the war. I had met up with a namesake of his, a concert pianist called Eric Harrison, who heard me in Portsmouth playing one of my own compositions. He said, 'That's rather good, you should send it to the Committee for the Promotion of New Music. My namesake Sidney

Harrison's on this committee, send it to him and see what he says.'

And that was the beginning of a lifelong friendship. He wrote back with two foolscap pages of criticism of the composition. He urged me to learn more about music, to co-operate with the Marine Band and write bits for them.

At the end of the war I came out and I had no job to go to, so I went to see Sidney Harrison and he said, 'You've got to take up music.' I said, 'But I've never had any training, I can't take up music.' He said, 'Yes you must, it's your talent, you must use it. I'll arrange an interview for you at the Guildhall School of Music. You must see the Principal and play him your compositions.' I did; he listened to them all and agreed to take me on as a composition student. I got a government grant, because I was an ex-serviceman, and I studied for three years.

How important do you think a mentor is, at some stage, in the life of a successful person?

In my case I think it was terribly important because Sidney put me on the right lines, was a great source of encouragement, and did it for no reason except that he wanted to help. And I couldn't pay him back; I've never been able to pay him back, except maybe by helping young people myself. I think older people should help young people; I think that's part of nature, and Sidney did a great job with me.

Then when you came out of the Guildhall School of Music, you worked in the BBC Music Library. What kind of a job was that? Was that a menial job? Were you right at the bottom of the ladder?

Oh absolutely, it was a job to give me money during the day, while I played music in the evenings. And it was very little money indeed. I looked after manuscripts and scores. If the

BBC Concert Orchestra wanted a particular work, I would look it out and make sure all the parts were there. It was a library job.

And how did you get the break with Parlophone EMI?

My fairy godfather again. It's a strange story, but Parlophone was a very small part of EMI in those days, and all the offices were at Abbey Road Studios.

The fellow who ran Parlophone was a chap called Oscar Preuss and he did it more or less by himself. He had an assistant, or rather a secretary, but no production assistant, and he was looking for one because he was 60, and he needed some help. He spoke to his friend, Victor Carne, who was, at that time, operatic producer for HMV and a great friend of Sidney Harrison. Victor, in turn, asked Sidney whether he knew of a young chap, with some musical talent, who might want a job at EMI? He gave him my address and out of the blue I got a letter asking if I would be interested in an interview for a post at EMI? So I cycled along, in my old naval greatcoat, and went to the interview and got the job at £7 4s 3d a week. That was 1950.

And in 1950, then, you suddenly found yourself working for Parlophone, making Noddy records.

Well, all sorts of records. To begin with I was put on the classical end of Parlophone, and because I'd taken up the oboe at the Guildhall, I was put in charge of a group called the London Baroque Ensemble, which specialized in Baroque music and woodwind music in particular – things like Mozart's Serenades.

We had the most wonderful musicians, and so when I started producing it was just supervision of the musicians. But, after a while, you begin to realize that you can influence things a little bit. I worked with people like Adrian Boult and Charles Mackerras and, at the same time, Oscar was offloading more and more stuff onto me. It was a label that did everything – classical music, jazz, children's records. I did little Noddy along with all the other things and met Enid Blyton.

Did you feel, at any stage, 'Hang on a second, why am I doing this? I want to do grander, greater, bigger, better things?'

Well to begin with it was a job which gave me more money and, again, enabled me to play in the evenings, and it was a kind of stepping stone to the ideal of being able to write music for film or concert performance. But as I got into it I became more and more fascinated by it and from 1950 through to 1955 I learned my craft. What's more I was losing my ambition to be Rachmaninoff II, and began to realize that I was probably better at telling people what to do rather than doing it myself.

By the time 1955 came along, I was virtually doing everything for the label. Oscar reached the age of 65 and retired and I thought someone else would be brought in above me. To my astonishment they gave me the job and I was head of Parlophone, at the age of 29. No one that young had ever been in charge of a label.

But what did that do to you, achieving such high success, so early? Did that change you in any way?

No, because it was all a gradual process. I mean by 1955 I was already making my own mark in records; I had started recording the top comedians, which became one of my specialist areas.

I worked with Peter Sellers, Spike Milligan, The Alberts, then Charlie Drake, Bernard Cribbins and Rolf Harris. I went to watch Michael Flanders and Donald Swan; I thought they were marvellous, and I made their albums. Later on I recorded the *Beyond the Fringe* people, Alan Bennett, Dudley Moore, Jonathan Miller and Peter Cook.

Did you ever feel, with that, that you were starting to move away from the musical sphere into speech production?

I think the two are entwined. One of the jobs that Oscar gave me when I was quite young, maybe two or three years into my career, was handling *School for Scandal* with Ralph Richardson, Edith Sitwell and Max Adrian. It was all part of the drama of recording, and I realized that we were painting pictures in sound and music, and words were all part of that.

Whether it was spoken words, sung words or music, you were evoking a world where if you could shut your eyes and listen to what you were doing, you could see things. And that was the way I always approached recording.

Then the Beatles came along and they had been rejected by everybody else. What made you think that the Beatles were worth running with?

Well we are onto 1962 now; it was in January 1962 that I first met Brian Epstein. I had a number two record with Jim Dale and I had a number one with the Temperance Seven – 'You're Driving Me Crazy' – but I was still looking for something. I was looking for an easy way of making hit records. I was very envious of my friend and co-producer on the Columbia label – Norrie Paramor. He had a young guy, Harry Webb, who became Cliff Richard, who seemed to be a great hit. It seemed almost effortless for Norrie; all he had to do was find a half decent song and because of the following for this chap, he had hit after hit. I thought, 'I must try some of this.'

So I was looking for something special, and the reason I met Brian Epstein was that I had received a phone call from a music publisher friend who worked for EMI, called Sid

Coleman. He'd met Brian because Brian had taken a tape into HMV Oxford Street to get some discs made for demonstration, and he had confessed to Sid that he'd seen everybody in the recording business and he was very dispirited.

Sid said, 'Have you been to EMI?' And Brian said, 'Yes, I've been round there and they've turned me down.' He said, 'Well, did you see George Martin there, he runs the Parlophone label?' He said, 'Parlophone, never heard of it.' Sid said, 'It's a kind of jazz/comedy label.' Brian knew he'd hit the all-time low, he'd been turned down by HMV, Columbia, Decca, Phillips, Pye, everybody and he didn't know where to go. So he said, 'If you can fix up for me to see him, I'd be grateful.'

Brian turned up with these records that he'd had cut at HMV and gave me the name of the group that he had, which I thought was a terrible name, Beatles, what an awful pun that was. Anyway I listened to it and the stuff was not very good, but he was so enthusiastic about his boys, as he called them; they were going to be good, they were going to be big.

Well, the quality wasn't very good. The songs weren't very good, the performances were rough. But there was something there. It was quite intriguing, a different sound. It certainly wasn't Cliff Richard, it was a bit rough and ready, but raw. So I said to Brian, 'Look, I can't judge on these demos, if you want me to be seriously interested in this group – the Beatles do you call them? – well bring them down – where are they, Liverpool? – bring them down to London and I'll listen to them in the studio.' And he groaned. He'd gone this route before, and now he had to go back to the Beatles and tell them that they had to come down again and go through the same routine.

They had a booking in Germany so we didn't fix a time until a couple of months later, and it was no skin off my nose. I thought it was an interesting possibility, but it was nothing vital.

When they eventually came into the studio, I spent three hours with them, and I fell in love with them. I thought they were terrific. I didn't fall in love with their music at first, I had to get into that, but as people they had great charisma. And they knew me and they knew all the records I'd made.

They were great fans of the Goons and Peter Sellers, and people like that, and we hit it off right away. They were very cheeky, which I quite liked, I mean there's the well-worn story about George Harrison. After the first take, I brought them into the control room and said, 'Look, this is what we've done with your sound, have a listen to it and tell me if there's anything you don't like.' George looked at me and said, 'Well I don't like your tie for a start.' That's absolutely true. The others pummelled him and said, 'You don't do that, he's an important guy.' I thought it was terribly funny.

So you liked them personally. But you can't allow your personal feelings to cloud your professional judgement, or can you?

Well you have gut feelings, and I had a gut feeling about them. My rationale was, if they have this effect on me, they are going to have a similar effect on people when they perform, if the music is good enough.

So to the extent that luck plays a part in success, the Beatles might never have happened if it hadn't been for that meeting with you?

Yes, it's probably true to say that.

So success is therefore dependent, not on innate talent, but on the breaks and the luck that you get, as you proceed through life?

It is, you've got to be lucky, but you also tend to make your own luck. As you go through life, every so often you come to a crossroads or a fork in the road and you take one way or the other way, and you try to judge which is the best way to go. Sometimes you take the wrong one, sometimes you take the right one, but the opportunities are always there. If you grasp them, then you get success. It's pretty nebulous stuff, but it is true.

Just after you gave the Beatles their big break, you had a major row with the company you were working for, and you walked out. What was that about?

Money. In fact, it was a long time after that. I left the company in 1965. I'd been thinking about leaving EMI before the Beatles came along. I actually signed a new contract in January 1962, for three years, but I was reluctant to do so.

For years I'd been saying that the people who made the records ought to have a commission. The artists got a royalty and the salesmen got their commission but we got nothing. Things finally came to a head in Christmas 1964, after we'd had a tremendously successful time.

Everybody got their Christmas bonus, which I think was about four days' pay – EMI were not renowned for being generous – but I didn't get mine. I couldn't understand, there must have been some mistake, so I rang up the accounts department and asked what had happened to it. They said, 'Oh, you don't get one now.' I said, 'I don't? Why not?' 'Well, you're over the £3000 limit. You're in a management class now, you are getting £3200 a year, people at that level don't get bonuses.' I was furious. That year we'd had number ones all over the place; we'd made millions for the company and I got no lousy bonus. So I was really rather angry.

But then you took the decision to go out on your own. It was based on anger, but there must have been a consideration of the risk involved, because even though you didn't get your bonus, you were in a secure job?

It was a gamble, but I guess I insured myself against the gamble to some extent. I was so determined to start my own production company that I invited three other people to join me, Ron Richards, my assistant at Parlophone, John Burgess, the assistant of my Columbia mate, Norman Newell, and Peter Sullivan, who had been assistant at HMV and had gone to Decca. They were all hit-makers, so between us we formed a pretty formidable combination. They were younger than I was, and I thought, they could carry me into my old age. It wasn't to be, but Peter recorded Engelbert Humperdinck and Tom Jones. John Burgess recorded Manfred Mann, Adam Faith and John Barry. Ron Richards had the Hollies. We had quite a team of hit artists between us. So we formed our new company and it was an adventure. I thought, 'If the worst comes to the worst, I can always get another job somewhere else.'

What do you regard as your greatest successes?

Well, the Beatles, obviously, come pretty high on that list in terms of financial success. Even recently, I've been astonished to see how well *The Beatles Anthology* has sold. Each double album has been number one in America, within a 12-month period, and so far we've sold about 14 million albums.

Talking about your successes, you were saying the Beatles, obviously. Any others?

Yes, I like to think that what we did in terms of making sound imagery, all the comedy work that I did with Peter Sellers and Peter Ustinov and those kind of people. I think that established a form of recording which, to me, was invaluable in making a Beatles record. I also like to think that the studios I've built have been a big success too. Air Studios in

Hampstead is the last I'll ever build, but I think it's probably the best studio there is and I'm rather proud of it.

Failures, and how did you recover from them?

Well the biggest failure in my life, I suppose, was my first marriage. The children of that marriage had to bear the brunt of that and I have always felt guilty. But you mustn't look back too much. Of course I've had lots of little failures. You record someone and think they are going to be great and they don't happen. Everything is a mixture of failure and success, and you just have to make sure that the successes outweigh the failures.

And the rewards of success have been fair, in your judgement? Or could you have made more from your success, financially?

Financially, I could have made a fortune, but that's not the point. You know you can only drive one car at a time. Most of the record producers that I know are much better off than I am. If you take someone like Dave Stewart, for example, he is probably worth about 25 times what I'm worth, but that doesn't matter. That doesn't worry me at all. I've been terribly lucky because I've always had plenty to live on, or rather enough to live on. And I've been able to provide for my family and send the children to good schools, and I've been honoured. I've really been very, very lucky indeed.

How do you get the balance right? What advice would you give to people about getting the balance right between the desire for financial independence, which a lot of success can bring you, and getting your own life in the right kind of balance?

I think you always must ask yourself whether you are getting what you want. If you just want success and money, then remember that you can end up being unsatisfied at the end of it. I think that you must remember that life is a balance, and life is giving as well as taking. In fact it should be more giving than taking, and a lot of people forget that. A lot of people just take.

What were the precise processes by which success came about for the Beatles, because you told them at first what they should do, but then you said it got round to the stage where they started telling you what to do. What was the balance between those two?

Well the success came by picking the right song and making the right arrangement for it. In the early days the success was in a succession of singles; the first album was done in a day, and it was just a recital of their songs. Success didn't really happen until that magic moment when we knew we were number one in America.

From that moment on it seemed they were able to write better songs each time, and they wrote different songs each time. They didn't write the same song over and over again. There was a big change-round about the time of *Rubber Soul. Rubber Soul* and *Revolver* are a couple of my favourite albums, and I suppose the apogée of it all was *Sergeant Pepper* – that really was painting pictures in sound.

Certainly their genius was manifest by this time, but they still needed direction and shaping, and we had become a very solid team. On the floor of the studio there were five people involved, the four Beatles and myself, all with good ideas, exchanging them, considering them and rejecting them, but every voice was equal.

Don't you have one person who is in control in an operation like that, who takes the final decision? Or can it evolve in the way you suggest?

It evolved very happily with us because, generally speaking, I would lean towards the person who'd written the song. He and I would be the decision-makers, but we would listen to the other people's ideas. So if it was John's song, he and I would decide how it would be, with input from the others. The same applied if it was Paul's song, and so on. Later on, there was an unhappy time with John who didn't like production techniques too much, but he was going through an unhappy time anyway, a very druggy period.

This was a time when he was also fighting with the others, but generally speaking our co-operation was a very happy one. And when, eventually, we came back and made the final record, *Abbey Road*, it was like the old days and John was his old self.

If you are successful, have you got to be prepared for your degree of control to ebb and flow?

Yes, and in my job you've got to be very tactful and very patient, and you've got to wait. You have to be like the Chinese proverb, you've got to sway with the wind and not break. And I think if you do that, then you see things through and you're able to get your own way, while other people still think they've got their way. That's the important thing.

What are the pressures of success?

Exhaustion. You have to pace yourself, you have to have a good constitution, you mustn't burn the candle at both ends. There are dreadful pressures on the young nowadays to experiment with drugs, and I can't impress that upon young people enough how dangerous these are. They are such a seduction and they are so destructive.

Have you seen pop groups simply disintegrate because of drugs?

I've seen people die because of them, and I've seen people become old men before their time. The ravages of drugs are awful. Of those who've indulged, some have seen the light in time, and there are quite a few of them who have survived, but it's better not to start in the first place.

You once said, 'Our civilisation builds up idols and icons and then tears them apart when it discovers they're not idols anymore.' Now, what did you mean by that and is that an inevitable part of success?

Yes, because everything's a bit of a myth really. We're all human beings, everyone you know. I was talking to Paul about this once, and we were discussing our past and looking at the images of 1964 and '65 and he said, 'You know, it's like it happened to other people, isn't it? It's like we're watching puppets, it is us but it's the images that other people see that aren't us. We know what we are because we're just human beings. You know, the Queen goes to the toilet like you do.' It's true, you know, we're just human beings.

How did you avoid the tearing apart process? Because that's never really happened, has it?

Again, I think my wife had a lot to do with it. I think that she could see when the strain became too great and she was able to warn me that I must pace myself and take it easy.

You've also said, that all creative people go through a period of self-disgust. Now what did you mean by that and how do you recover? How do you pull out of that period?

The process of creation, I suppose, is very much a lonely affair and you can get yourself into a situation where you get carried away with your own thoughts and you think you're brilliant and then you suddenly realize that you may be kidding yourself, and you start worrying about that and saying, 'Am I what I think I am?' You have moments of self-doubt and they, in turn, can become tremendous troughs of despondency.

So how do you pull back from those?

I think you have to take the broad view; you have to look at yourself and say, 'Well, in the end nothing really matters. Absolutely nothing. What are we for heavens sake? We are tiny grains of sand in the Universe; we are so insignificant and yet we're worried about whether our record's going to make it to the top ten or not. For God sake, in a few years time, all this will be forgotten, we're just a passing bit of dust.' If you can take that view then it certainly brings you down to earth.

It's a very difficult view to take, because at the time your priority, your obsession, if you like, is this particular musical project you're working on?

Of course, but you've got to level yourself. You've got to get things in perspective. Nothing is really that important. Very few of us are prime ministers about to go to war with another country. Most of the decisions we take are very personal ones and they only affect the little people around us. They are not big deals.

So to be able to think like that, do you have to have a kind of inner calm, a sort of equilibrium which enables you to ride across those troughs, or indeed not even to have them at all?

I think you have to have an inner calm; I think you have to try to adopt it and many people have different ways of doing this. George Harrison is a great believer in transcendental meditation and he's a believer in many of the cults of the Far

East. When I was ill he came to see me and brought with him a lovely bunch of flowers and a little wooden carving of the God Ganesh, you know, the elephant one. And he said, 'Put him by your bed and look at him before you go to bed and you will be all right.' He had this enormous belief. Well, Ganesh is still by my bed and that's fine.

And did you look at it every day?

I do look at him from time to time, but no, I'm a Christian and I do believe in God. I think if you have that faith it helps.

Has religion been a part of your success?

Religion's a nasty word to me. I hate organized religion. I think most of the religions have failed. I think the Church of England has some very good people in it, but as an organization, it's not too good. And the Roman Catholic faith has got so many paradoxes in it that it doesn't serve most people. I think you've got to build up your own inner faith.

And that can take whatever form you like, really?

Yes, I mean in my case it's taken a lifetime to come about, but I do believe that there is a great Being and I think that we are terribly, terribly insignificant people. I think if you have that humbleness, it does help.

You once said failure and success can both be traps. What did you mean by that?

The trap is in getting too big for your boots. In the entertainment world it's legion. I've seen so many people who, because they are talented, become very successful, and because they become very successful they are idolized, and because they are idolized they become monsters.

I suppose the supreme example of that was Peter Sellers, who was a dear chap and, in the early days of the Goons, he was enormous fun, but then he became a big film star. He had a herd of sycophants who were always telling him how marvellous he was and consequently he came to believe it and became very difficult when he was working on the film set. He indulged in things he shouldn't do and he died much too young. He came to sec me – I was living in America in 1976, I think it was – and spent the day with me. He was already ill, he'd already had a heart attack and he now was on his last wife, whom he'd just met, Lynn Frederick, and I felt awfully sorry for him because he wasn't the man that I knew. We had a very nice time together, we spent the whole afternoon by the pool and we had dinner in the evening, but there was a feeling of loss somehow, and it was a great shame.

How could that have been stopped, that process with him?

If he hadn't listened to so many people, saying how good he was and if, when he asked a person's opinion they had told the truth instead of just giving him the eternal feed. It's always difficult.

With Paul McCartney or John Lennon, for example, most of their songs were brilliant, but if there was a song I didn't think was very good, I would tell them so. But if *you* were asked by Paul McCartney or George Michael or someone like that to produce his record and you didn't think much of the song, would you tell him? Would you say, 'I'm sorry, I don't think that song's very good, Paul'? It needs a lot of nerve and Paul's got to have respect for that person to be able to take the criticism. In the later stages I don't think Peter Sellers was ever told that that didn't work, or that wasn't funny. Or if he was, it probably never got through to him.

Is it more or less difficult to achieve musical success now?

It depends what you mean by musical success. I think in the pop world it's a much bigger lottery than it used to be and I don't think music has got a great deal to do with it. Visual image is the most important thing of all.

Do you regret that?

Yes I do. I think that people now don't listen with their ears, they listen with their eyes. We are so conditioned by the television screen that anything that comes on it that is attractive visually, is accepted. And if the image is right, then records will sell.

So the image, what appears on the screen, can override the intrinsic musical quality of a record. In other words, a bad record can sell because of a great image?

Absolutely. I think this is one of the reasons why we don't have the sort of music that is likely to last very long. In the early days of the Beatles, although they had charisma and a good image, it wasn't the vision that sold, it was the sound they were making. But I don't think Michael Jackson would've been as big as he is without the benefit of his videos.

What are the ingredients of a successful song?

It's so difficult to give a formula for it. If I knew the answer, I'd be writing them all the time. A memorable melody, a meaningful lyric, attractive harmonies that don't go down the well-worn route, and a very catchy rhythm. I think those are some of the ingredients, anyway.

Is it more and more difficult to write something that is new and original because, in a sense, every sequence of notes has been written before in some form or another?

That's true, but that's always been true. Gershwin had the same problem. The notes were still the same 12 notes on the scale and he came up with 'Summer Time'; nobody had thought of that one before. And when Paul woke up and played 'Yesterday', no one had thought of that one either, but he thought they had. No, it's possible. I don't think it's any more difficult than it has been, but it is difficult.

If you were setting up a really successful group or singer now, how would you set about that?

Well being very cynical about it, it would have to be a manufactured job. And I would choose a group of people who were very attractive to look at, whether they're male or female. I would get them choreographed so that their movements were very attractive, also hip, and would appeal to young people. I would find a song that was well written and with a good hook. I would get them to sing it well, and if they didn't sing it well I'd even substitute really good singers who could, and pretend that they had done it. Then I would sell it, market it mercilessly, until it became a hit. That's, of course, being very cynical.

Are there any people, big or small, past or present, who you really admire? People who you think have reached the pinnacle of success, in any field? Who are your heroes?

Oh, I've got lots of heroes. In fact I'm making an album of heroes at the moment. I was with one of my heroes yesterday, Sean Connery. I think he's such a magnificent character. He's got enormous charisma. He is Mr Scotland to me, he's done a lot for Scotland, and I think he ought to be Sir Sean Connery. He's just one of my heroes. There are lots of people in America that I've never met, that I regard as heroes. I think Goldie Hawn is wonderful.

Those are present day people, anyone in history?

Well the inevitable Winston Churchill; he was a hero, because I remember, as a child, everyone being moved by what he did. There aren't many politicians who are heroes, and a lot of my heroes are people who aren't well known, people with great courage who've gone through some dreadful times. They've coped with grief, or they've coped with disability and setbacks with great cheer.

There was a woman, for example, in my village, who is now dead; she was crippled almost from birth and she was in a wheelchair all her life. But she raised children and she always had a smile on her face; she had nothing. We used to take our children down to her cottage and she was always full of life and so delighted to see us, and the sun would shine. When you went to see her and spoke with her, you felt better for it. She was a wonderful woman. There are people like that.

Success in others arouses conflicting emotions, ranging from admiration, right through to envy. Why do you think it should have such a different reaction amongst people?

Well I suppose that some people think that success is not deserved, in which case their envy becomes rather rank. In this country we do tend to be a little bit envious. There's the old joke about the difference between Americans and English in that if an Englishman sees someone in a Rolls Royce, his immediate reaction is, 'Damn bureaucrat in a flash car.' And if it happened in America, the fellow would say,

'Wonderful car that, I'm going to have one of those one day.' There is that kind of difference, a kind of envy in our make-up that is none too attractive.

What do you think are the greatest enemies of success?

The greatest enemies of success are probably sloth, indolence and a lack of care for other people.

Do you think success brings obligations to the rest of society in its wake?

No question about it. I think that the whole point about success should be to set an example to other people, and to help other people. I think without that, it's empty.

Have you any frustrated ambitions?

Not really, no. I'm an old man now and I've been jolly lucky. There is perhaps one frustrated ambition, I haven't yet managed to clear all the balls on a snooker table.

Has success changed you at all?

I hope not. I don't know, you'd have to ask other people that.

But do you feel within yourself, that there has been some kind of a change as you've become more and more successful? Or there was that kind of a change, at some stage in your life.

I honestly don't think so. I mean I still have the same friends I had. As I've got older, I might have become a little more self-assured than I was, but I hope I haven't changed very much.

What's the greatest pleasure you've had from your success?

Being able to enjoy the trappings of success. Being able to take my wife out to dinner in a nice restaurant without having to worry about whether I can pay the gas bill or not. That's one of them. And also having a good circle of friends, people are everything.

If you could gather together, in one room, all the young people poised above the bottom rung of the ladder, wanting to make a career, whether it be in front of the microphone or behind the microphone, as you have, what advice would you give them, to enable them to stand a fair chance of becoming as successful as you've been?

Master your craft; whatever it is, whether you're a carpenter or a soprano, master your craft. Work hard and learn and take advice from the people who know. Being an apprentice, you've got to learn your trade, whatever it is, in any walk of life. And then, along with that, be true to yourself; don't go astray. Always ask yourself if you're doing the right thing for yourself and for other people. Don't do things just because other people do them, don't be led astray. Follow your own path, keep going at it and don't let go. Keep persevering. It's the people who give up who fail. The people who succeed are those people who are tenacious, who hang on and say, 'I can make it, I will make it.'

And how do you handle the critics? How do you handle the inevitable knocks on your path through life?

You get them, you're bound to get them, but you deal with the critics by saying, 'Are they being honest? Are they being true? Are these things I should correct?' If they are, correct them. If they're not, they're being malicious, forget them. It's down to you. You have to make up your own mind, you have to find your own way, there's no other way.

And if someone wanted to move behind the scenes in the music business and become a music producer – is there anything specific that they ought to do? Any specific course that they ought to go on, or I mean is it not like that anymore?

Courses do help, but it's more difficult now than it's ever been because the competition is so great. When I started I was terribly lucky; there were only a handful of people who made records in the country. And now I think every third person is a record producer. Again, you have to learn your craft, and by that you have to get yourself into a recording studio and you have to start watching other people doing it. But I would urge people not to do it, because it's a very overcrowded profession. Try and choose a career that isn't quite so competitive and then work at it.

So you are basically saying, don't come on board the ship that has been so successful for me?

I am actually, because everybody is already on board and the whole ship is sinking.

And what about the singing front? People who are in front of the microphone – what advice would you give to them, on top of the general principles that you've outlined?

Well, obviously try and do your very best. Try not to get nervous; try to listen to yourself rather than to other people; don't worry about what other people are doing and listening to; don't be distracted; don't, while you're performing, think, 'Is he looking at that mole on my left cheek?' It's easy for me to say this, and this is why being a producer is easier than being a performer, but I remember what it was like when I played the oboe at a music exam. I was so nervous that my fingers began to sweat and the sweat ran down the keys of my oboe and my fingers slipped on the keys, which made me make mistakes, which made me more nervous, which made me sweat more. It's very difficult to overcome that kind of dreadful fear.

But how do you overcome it?

I didn't. I gave it up and did something else.

But from what you have observed of artists out there, a lot would go through that same kind of nervous tension.

Everyone does and it doesn't matter who it is. If you talk to Kenneth Branagh, Emma Thompson, Anthony Hopkins, they will all admit that they get scared witless sometimes; they all do.

So how do you get over it?

You take heart from the fact that everybody goes through it and say, 'I'm going to overcome it as they did.' And you just have to buckle your belt a bit tighter and stiffen the sinews. It's a discipline. You've got to learn it, you've got to really drill yourself into it.

One final question. When your time comes to leave this planet, what would you like people to say about you?

He went an awful long way on a very thin talent.

What do you think they will say?

I've no idea. I hope they will say he was a nice man who loved other people. That's what I'd like it to be.

ANITA RODDICK

Body Shop founder Anita Roddick has spent most of her life challenging the way people think. In setting up an eco-friendly beauty products empire that straddles the world, she has been the living embodiment of one of her most famous advertising slogans – 'if you think you're too small to be effective, try going to bed with a mosquito.'

She opened an 'exhausting' café/restaurant which 'taught her how to run a business'. Then, in 1976, she tried to raise a £4,000 bank loan to start the Body Shop, but was turned down. 'The banks were useless at the start,' she says, 'and still are. It's easier for a woman to raise money for her new kitchen cabinet, or even a car, than for a business enterprise.' So her husband, Gordon, borrowed the money – and gave it to her. Later, she could only raise money for expansion by giving away 50 per cent of the company in return – a move that she (but not the lucky investor!) now regrets.

She measures her company each year 'by how brave we've been' – and needed lots of bravery to deal with a potentially hugely damaging article attacking the Body Shop's ethos and methods. She talks here of how she used 'reputation management' to counter this 'corporate stalker', of how the allegations were challenged 'word for word'; and of 'the intimacy approach', writing to every single shop to restore 'the sense of family' – a technique she used again when threatened with a franchisee rebellion.

Anita Roddick, what is your definition of success?

I want to define success by redefining it. For me it isn't that solely mythical definition: glamour, allure, power of wealth, and the privilege from care. Any definition of success should be personal because it's so transitory. It's about shaping my own destiny.

If you'd have asked me this question 20 years ago, my definition of success would have been to have earned enough money to keep the kids fed. Ten years ago, it would have been to see how far the idea of The Body Shop could go? I would have measured it by how many people I employed, or how many stores are open, or whether we could open a store in another country?

What you're saying is that you start off in the very early stages, having relatively short-term materialistic ambitions, but as you're more successful you can then embrace wider concepts?

Yes, that's it in a nutshell, but when you're dealing with the question of success you have to deal with the personality of the people you're talking to. My entrepreneurial style is quite pathological. An entrepreneur is very enthusiastic and dances to a different drum beat, but never considers success as something which equates to personal wealth; that never enters our consciousness. We have incredible enthusiasm, and I think part of the success of any entrepreneur is energy. If one has that energy one can create a wonderful enthusiasm. Entrepreneurs have this real belief that their lives are about service and leadership.

So you don't believe that anyone seeking success is driven in any way by financial considerations?

I don't know about anybody else, but that's certainly not the case as far as I'm concerned. I'm wealthy, I've been wealthy for ten years. I've been free from hunger all my life: my life has been about challenging myself; it's been about a journey; it's been about the romance of that journey, the achievement of success.

What are the qualities that people need, to stand a reasonable chance of being successful?

You've got to be energetic. You've got to have a passion which comes from every tentacle of your body, and you've got to make that passion a reality. You have to constantly visualize the possible. I think if you have this passion for what you want to do, it creates a vision in your head which becomes the present. It's never something you aspire to, it *is* the present, and therefore you never see any problems. And no entrepreneur that I've ever met has ever seen a problem.

Are you born with this passion, or can you learn it?

No. It's not inherent, it's a learned state. I think the environment that you're growing up in is instrumental. If you look at most entrepreneurs, what do they have in common? Most of them have understood a sense of loss. They've been pushed out of childhood and rather than entering adulthood, they became providers. In my case my father died. We were an immigrant family in which every member *had* to work so we were always outside the stream: we never smelt the same as anybody; we stank of garlic; we never spoke the same; we were much more full of Italian *brio*; we were much more contradictory; we didn't have the sacred cows that other people had. So when you march to a different drum beat, you look at things in a different way – you're never part of the throng.

Was being an outsider a factor in the sense that outsiders have to try harder than people who are part of the mainstream?

Definitely. And the immigrant background that I had, instilled in me a sense that life was no more complicated than love and work. You had to work – even as a child – to earn enough money to keep the family going. We didn't have the constraints of class; we thought everything was possible, we didn't understand the class system here. And, as I mentioned before, we had energy and a secret ingredient, enthusiasm.

Were you an outsider at school as well?

Yes, but an outsider that knew how to work the system. I knew what people wanted at a really early age: people want to be told that they are remarkable, or that they are loved. From ten years old, I was the only student that rushed up to teachers to say, 'I love you, I've just learnt something new.' It was something that came from my mum who could hardly speak Italian and my grandmother who could hardly speak English: I told them how I loved what they were teaching me; I think that gave them a feeling that they were doing things. It wasn't manipulative, it was just this wonderful enthusiasm.

Were you a bit of loner?

No, I don't think so. I had the ability at an early age to attract this mischievous group of kids into my circle. We were respectful, but we were incredibly devious, as all kids are. If we didn't get things one way we got it our way.

And when you left school you wanted to go into drama because you'd done drama at school. So at that stage, your future career was totally unformed, in fact it wasn't even in your mind, was it?

I suppose it's all about what shaped you as a child. My parents were Italian. My culture was the radio and the cinema. Because we didn't have television, we went to the cinema five days a week. It bred this desire to be up there on the golden screen. I can project my own individuality or fashion somebody else's identity, but my mum couldn't understand my wish to go into drama. She wanted me to go into a profession; to be a teacher, a nurse or a secretary.

So you rebelled against her, in applying for drama college?

I don't think I rebelled against her; I just thought I was good at it. My first element of success was winning a talent competition. It was the most interesting thing the school have ever heard.

What was that talent competition?

Well, at 14, I was having this major love affair with the dead James Dean. I wanted to read everything he had read. He read Strindberg, I read Strindberg. He read Ibsen, I read Ibsen. He was in love with this particular soliloquy, the madman soliloquy from a Charles Dickens novel, so I copied that as well. I dressed like a madman, wrapped in chains. I did what Stanislavsky, the great Russian director, did; I opened the curtain with my back to the audience, started with this great blood-curdling scream, and then acted like a maniac. It was so intensely exciting and I won. So I knew the power of theatre then and I don't think it's ever left me.

And did you feel you liked an audience?

I was comfortable with an audience. I had no sense of fear as long as I knew something about what I was doing. Even today, standing in front of 10,000 people, which I do occasionally to give a lecture or a talk, holds no fear for me at all.

You'd set your heart on a drama career, but you were turned down by the Central School of Speech and Drama. That was clearly a setback, how did you deal with that within yourself?

I thought, 'Where's my next audience?' If I wanted to make the most of my ability to project myself, the best thing in the world was to be a teacher. So there I was, a working-class kid going to a very middle-class teacher training college for three years, and then I became a teacher. I wanted to project myself onto the school room; and I did. It was hugely entertaining. For example, I dragged – this was in the 1960s so you could do that then – a group of kids who were studying O-level history on the First World War to France. We hitched there and slept in the trenches that still remained. We read Rupert Brooke poems. We acted out Joan Littlewood's *Oh! What a Lovely War*. I can't imagine any teacher being able to do that nowadays. But that was my style of teaching; it was all experiential.

You were clearly enjoying teaching, why did you stop?

I think it's about limitations; my limitation was the classroom. I was half a dozen years older than the kids I was teaching. The only difference between them and myself was that I was one side of the desk and they were the other.

One of the great things about the early 1960s was this new-found freedom to travel, especially as a working-class student. Student loans enabled students to travel, and travelling for me was like a university without walls; it always provided insights. I travelled to Paris and I lived in Paris; I worked for the United Nations in Geneva; I spent a year travelling around the Indian Ocean Islands and Pacific Islands, living with pre-industrial groups, fishing groups – that's when I first understood the power of community and a world beyond our Western notion, and the role women could play in it. It was education through experience, and it was where I got the ideas for The Body Shop.

Was The Body Shop in your mind at this stage?

No. I wanted to be a television director, a magnificent teacher, or whatever. I had no idea – all I wanted to do was to experience as much as I could.

So at this stage you were still uncertain as to what your future career would be? You were trying out lots of things and visiting all kinds of different places. You went on the hippie trail, but then you came back and started an Italian restaurant in Littlehampton.

Well it was hardly an Italian restaurant. It started as a health-food café in Littlehampton, but after no time I realized we were going to go bankrupt. So we brought in a chip fryer, hamburgers and made pastas. I mean I remember one guy coming up and saying, 'Could I have a quick Lorraine and a glass of rosy wine?' But we had a sense of style: you cannot talk about success if you don't involve the words aesthetics and ethics, because to deny yourself the sense of delight and pleasure around whatever you do, is to deny one of the great aspects of who you are as an individual. I styled everything, and the café looked like a wonderful Victorian celebration of Littlehampton at the turn of the century. We had music, but what's more, a real understanding of community.

Was it a financial success?

Yes. And not only was it a financial success, it allowed my husband, Gordon, to go off for two years to ride this horse across South America. It allowed me the freedom to set up something which was going to be really small and controllable, The Body Shop, and it also gave me an enormous sense of understanding as to how to run a business. Nobody, but nobody works as hard as somebody running a restaurant because you're working in other peoples' leisure time, and you're dealing with culture; you're dealing with a sense of aesthetics; you're dealing with service; you're dealing with preparation; you're dealing people's satisfaction. Eating is one of the greatest satisfactions, if you don't get it right, you're in trouble. And it's unbelievably exhausting; I've never been more tired in my life, closing that café or that restaurant at night – at 11 o'clock, night after night. You go straight to bed and you can't get up in the morning because your legs are so damned exhausted. I can't understand how anybody wants to open up a restaurant!

So did you open up the first Body Shop to escape from the pressure of the restaurant?

Yes, I opened up The Body Shop because Gordon wanted to go away. I wanted a nice, easy, controllable nine-to-five, pick-up-the kids-from-school existence.

And what was the original concept of The Body Shop?

It was all about education through experience, and women are really good at this; understanding what they are interested in. During my years of travelling, I picked up on so many ideas from people that I'd lived with – for example, in Tahiti the women wouldn't eat cocoa butter, they'd just rub it on their bodies and their skin was like silk. So my experiences with people from other cultures taught me things like that. I was also dissatisfied and dissatisfaction is a primary mover for energy; I used to go into a local chemist and only be able to buy this gallon of shampoo, and I used to think to myself, 'Why can't I have a small bottle? Why can't I refill it?' Simple questions like that. And the entrepreneur in me would say, 'Why not, why can't you?' That dissatisfaction gave me the energy to set it up.

And did you think, at that stage, 'This is the start of an empire'? You only had one shop didn't you?

I never think big, I just think better, or more exciting. The nature of size is of no interest to me at all. The barometers of measurement for me are, is it better? is it more exciting? Until Gordon came back from the trip, it was just a livelihood. I just had this energy and opened up another shop and was fortunate enough to find somebody to loan me some money to do it.

And when you were trying to raise the money for the initial Body Shop, did you find the bank helpful?

Useless. And 20 years later they're still as bad. It is still easier for a woman to raise money for her new kitchen cabinet or even a car, than it is for a business enterprise. It's seduction and that's wrong, because you're seduced into believing that the banks are really supportive of women; they're not, especially if they're mothers. It's a very patriarchal system, not unlike the military. In 20 years, I have never met a bank manger who has the excitement and the *brio* of an entrepreneur. They're good housekeepers, they protect themselves.

After you opened your first shop and it was starting to make money, you decided to open a second. Did you go to the bank before anybody else to see if you could raise money? What was their reaction?

The first time I went, they said no to me, and so my husband returned. They gave Gordon the money and he gave it to me. It's pathetic, but that's how it was. When I wanted to open up my second store, there was no way I was going to go to the bank. I'd only been trading for six months, we didn't know whether it was going to work. It could just be a fad, nobody had done this type of stuff before, and we didn't know whether it was going to work. So I had to find a private investor.

And you had to give away a slice of the business because of that.

I gave 50 per cent of it away. And that's been one of the biggest dilemmas for people reading the history of my company. 'How could you have done it?' I had no problem with it, because the accumulation of wealth is of no importance to me. Giving my wealth away, however, is of major importance to me: how I give it away, when I give it away, why I give away. So I had no problem with that, but, yes, 50 per cent is sitting in somebody else's pocket.

What was the trigger for the massive expansion of The Body Shop?

The trigger was self-financing. We didn't have any more money. Gordon came back and he said, 'We've got two stores, but how are we going to fund anybody else or anything else?' But luckily at that time people were coming along and saying, 'This is a good idea.' Women were coming to The Body Shop in Brighton and saying, 'I like this. I could do this. I could fill the bottles in the back, and hand-write the labels.' It was like a cottage industry, but it was fun. We had this intimacy, and we were thankful if anybody came along. It wasn't until a couple of years later that we started to embrace the concept of franchising. Then, anybody would come along, put the products in the back of their car, and sell them from barges and market stalls. So the business really defined itself about four or five years later when we suddenly realized we'd found something unique. We created this market; even though we didn't know what marketing was.

When did all this formulate into a business plan?

We started to get really serious about five or six years later, especially when we opened up in Covent Garden. There was this new shopping experience occurring in England, which didn't solely include the big retailers. We suddenly realized we'd got something going here and that we had to take it seriously. But the real benchmark was when we decided to go public. We started to employ financial directors; we had to have a strategy plan. We had to grow up; we had to be professional; we had to have strong financial direction.

It's the bottom line the whole time.

Yes, and there is such a tyranny in the bottom line.

And yet, isn't that bottom line important? Apart from the fact that it determines the share price of your company, it actually dictates the extent to which you can use your profits to invest in expanding the business, and indeed to do all the other things that you want to do?

I agree with you, but you have to have a belief that your shareholders are *not* your financial investors; you have stakeholders, your employees, and I am more loyal to my employees than to any other group. You also have your customers, your suppliers. All of these peoples' livelihoods depend on you, so I want to equalize that level of responsibility to the importance of the financial investor.

Many of the investors are speculators. They only put a few pounds in our company for a nanosecond. When one talks about profit, one has to ask, 'Profit for whom?' How do my employees profit? How do the customers profit? Why do we only define profit as a financial profit? If we are to become visionaries in business, we are going to have to redefine words like profit. Does the environment profit by this obsession for growth? I'm now on that treadmill: how can I make my growth more responsible? How can I clean up the mess I create? How can I move towards sustainability? How can I move towards redefining the nature of business? It's a hard task to try and redefine that every day you're open for business.

As The Body Shop expanded and moved into America, you had a huge amount of praise and then, suddenly, there was this article in Business

Ethics, *a small-circulation magazine of 14,000, which rocked you back on your heels. Now what was your reaction, a, when that article appeared? and b, what did you decide to do about it?*

Well, we had a corporate stalker! This is not just a man who wrote an article because he felt he had something to say. He was a man who wanted to challenge the very heart of our business. If my company was a woman he'd be up in front of the High Courts. Even as we speak, he's trying to get articles in the *Guardian.* I don't know where he comes from, and I don't know the source of his income, all I know is his wife is vice-president of marketing for our biggest competitor in America.

It was the saddest time in my life because this article was placed in a friend's publication – we're all part of the Social Responsibility Movement in America – and she thought it was juicy enough and put it in because I reckon she needed to raise the circulation! The article was scathing; it was appalling. We tried to counteract the allegations made but we were seen as defensive. This huge web of assumptions was built around us, and we had to fight our way out of it.

What was more intriguing was what happened in England. We had 150 articles about us within a week – more than Bosnia. We had BBC TV, we had ITV, we had cameras, we had microphones. What were they looking for? Three gallons of shampoo that were leaked out into pipes in New Jersey. This is nothing compared to what goes on. It was the juiciest story they could find and we couldn't get our head around it. It was our darkest time because we lived on our radical reputation.

So how did you tackle it?

It was really interesting. We were camping out on the floor of our offices because our communication department had to be open 24 hours a day. We had to curb these stories which were going out internationally. I found intimacy was the only way to keep my sanity and my sense of reality. I wrote intimate faxes to every shop. It was like a diary of how I felt: how I had to rush out and get some pizzas; how we were camping out on the floor. I got letters back from our stores in Colorado, Taiwan, everywhere. That sense of being a family gave me great support. It was like grieving, and people were saying, 'Don't grieve, this is all right.'

That handles the emotional side, what did you do about the allegations?

We challenged them word for word, line by line. What was profoundly helpful for us, at that time, was the support that we had from Greenpeace, from Friends of the Earth, from Jonathan Porritt and Sara Parker. The people whose opinions we really valued are the people who understood the real essence of the values inherent in our company; we were amazed by the support.

Do you feel you've come through that now?

Yes. Now that people understand the pathology of the man who wrote the article. They understand where he comes from and what his agenda is.

Did you have a strategy for dealing with the media for countering all this? Because as you say, there were articles, or news reports, which were fairly hostile?

Yes, we had a great strategy, but it didn't appear to do us any good. For the first time in our lives we had to do reputation management. And when you're coming from a company like ours, its whole brand is its reputation, and its values. We had to learn fast. We had to deal with the detail, the minutiae, because this man was going back 20 years, inventing scenarios and making assumptions. People hated the fact that we defended ourselves. We lost our credibility, because we had been too defensive; it looked as though we could not handle criticism. I'm still confused about it all three years later, and yet, to this day, I would defend my company in exactly the same way against such an obsessive person.

Have you ever got to the stage where you thought, 'Things are so grim I've got to give up, I've got to go and try something else'?

My husband will say, 'When are we going to start having more fun again? When are we going to lighten up and be less tense?' The dilemma for me is that I don't know how to differentiate between enthusiasm and stress. I find it hard. My husband keeps on saying, 'Let's be a bit detached. We've got so many juicy projects, so much human rights campaigning to do.' But at the moment I don't feel I can do that, and when I do feel I can let go, then maybe I will. At the moment it's all so tense and vibrant.

What do you think is the difference between success, as seen in Britain and success in the United States?

I think there is such a poverty of praise in this country. I think they love to see you grow – and I know this is such a cliché – and then whack! I think it's to do with cynicism. And you have a double whammy if you're a woman because the female press do *not* support women in this country, and I don't know why, but it seems to happen that way. We don't know how to praise: we're cynical, so there's the problem.

In America and Canada, they just love the notion of breaking rules. They love the sense that you're inspiring; that you came from nowhere and did it. They have such a history of grassroot success; they celebrate that and warm towards you. There isn't this distance of observing over there, and they're much more in-your-face with it all. Here success is defined by the media, it is more prurient and alluring. It's to do with wealth and power, and if that's the only definition then I guess it will always be a dilemma for me because my definition is different.

Are there any other downsides to success?

Yes. On a personal level it is that people see you as an opportunity for furthering their own ideas. I get people coming up and saying, 'Can you read my business plan,' or, 'What do you think about this, what do you think about that?' You become a magnet. It's a constant strain. When I give talks I have to find a quick exit more often than not because the vast majority of people want to talk to you about themselves or what they're trying to do. It's as though they expect an instant answer, a soundbite, that will move them to success.

Does luck play a part in success?

I'm not sure. Opportunism does. I don't understand luck. I don't think that I've been lucky.

Being in the right place at the right time, getting an early loan, finding a partner?

Is that luck? I don't know. In 1976 nobody could have spelt the word environmentalism. We just had an antenna out there and knew who were the forerunner in the planet. The real wisdom-seekers of the planet were the environmental groups, and we just listened, and still do; they give us direction. We're opportunistic. We see an opportunity and go with it, but I don't think luck plays any part in our success.

Is image important to success?

I think so. For me the image of the company is really important. What people perceive when they think about us. My image is really important. I don't want to be seen as a cosmetic diva, wearing high heels and hobbling around with 18 inches of make-up. I want to be seen as an activist and approachable.

Success in others arouses a wide range of emotions from envy to outright admiration. Why should there be those vastly differing views of success? Is there something inside people that shapes whether they're envious or whether they admire, or is it a national characteristic?

It's the intangible rewards. For a lot of people those rewards mean that you have freedom from financial worry. And God, how many of us have gone through it and still worry about that? Also, the rewards that you can be in the best place at the best time; you have the freedom to be spontaneous. Envy is such a dark thing, a Western thing. We've shaped it; the media have shaped it in a different way. If you were to define success in other countries, it would be the ability to share, the ability to welcome your neighbour, the ability to welcome strangers.

Has success changed you at all?

It must have. If this hadn't happened 20 years ago, what would I be doing? It's given me the knowledge that I can be spontaneous. It's given me an immense sense of not being frightened about the word 'power'. Women are always frightened about power because they see how men have manipulated it and they want no part of it. Success has given me the ability to be influential, and the thing which I delight in more than anything else, the ability to be heard.

What do you think are the greatest enemies of success?

Lethargy, assumption.

In pursuit of success, have you ever done anything you'd wished you hadn't done?

Yes. Being so open to the press. I always think they will take me as I am, with the honesty that I offer and there will not be any manipulation.

But there is an argument that says, any publicity is good publicity?

Well that's an argument I do not believe in because the consequences can be incredibly painful.

But when you get criticism like that, what's the inner mechanism you have to deal with it? What technique do you use to steal yourself up to go out and face another day?

First of all, it's the knowledge that you know the criticism is not true. The sense that what drives you forward is something beyond yourself, and that it has been the passion since day one. Secondly, the support from the people whose opinions you respect. The people you benchmark against.

And they are better barometers than the media?

Oh yes, because the media have got to have a story that will sell; it has to be verbally cute or cynical.

If you could gather together all the young people in the world who look up to you as someone who they would like to become, running their own company, with all the concerns that you've got, but they're there with their feet on the bottom rung of the ladder, what advice would you give them?

First of all, keep it simple, ask questions; constantly ask questions. Look to people you admire and go straight to them and say, 'How do I do it. What advice can you give me?' We don't help in this country. We don't care about the young kids. I would encourage them to knock on the doors of people who could help them, with their skills or with their ideas. Secondly, if they want to set up their own companies, don't think 'business', think 'livelihoods'. We're being paralysed by the notion of setting up your own companies, or setting up your own businesses, forget that word. Think in terms of, 'How can I have a livelihood that gives me independence, freedom of spirit, and where I don't have to rely on anybody for a job?'

When your time comes to leave this life, what would you like people to say about you?

She challenged with enthusiasm.

And what about your famous mosquito slogan?

If you think you're too small to be effective, try going to bed with a mosquito!

BRUCE OLDFIELD

The man who has dressed some of the most beautiful women in the world believes that success is all about 'staying there'. 'Getting there is important, of course, but the great danger is that you're a one-night wonder.' That was just one of the lessons he learnt the hard way.

Certainly, his early life was far from easy. A Barnardos baby when just a day-and-a-half old, he grew up with a foster mother in Durham – 'in those days one of the few black kids in the North East.' Seven of them lived in a tiny two-up-two-down house with a 'no-flush' lavatory out the back. They were, he says, very poor, with the accompanying very low career expectations.

Maybe that was what drove him to be an early entrepreneur – organising lunchtime discos, getting refunds on empty bottles, selling chocolate biscuits at break and doing an evening paper round.

Throughout his schooldays he was a rebel and a troublemaker, once being sent back to Barnardos briefly when he was caught pinching sweets. But he doesn't believe in lingering regrets. 'Feeling sorry for yourself is a total waste of time – just get on with it.' Which perhaps explains why – after living with a stutter that lasted until he was 20 – he developed an inner confidence so strong that, in his early career, he was (he confesses) 'the most arrogant prat known to man'. And, even two decades of fame later, he nearly came a cropper once more, when the recession threatened his 'bulky and mismanaged' company with bankruptcy. His learning curve is tinged with cynicism – 'if the press like the collection, it won't sell.' He thinks editorial comment now counts for very little; it is advertising that brings in the customers.

Bruce Oldfield, what is your definition of success?

I think the definition of success has to be staying there – getting there's important obviously, but staying there, not being a one-night wonder, which is the great danger in fashion, in fact it's encouraged, I think.

Is it easier to achieve the sudden success than being successful for some period of time?

Exactly. As soon as I left college, I left St Martin's in 1973, I got all of the press coverage and my first show was in New York four months later, and I didn't even get a qualification, a degree; then it was two months in New York and back on the bus, because the things hadn't sold well enough. Americans don't invest very much in time, they want things to happen straight away, and if they don't you're out and the next one's in; it's a conveyer belt. I came down with a bump and I coasted for a while. My career's gone up and down, up and down, up and down, but it's always been a question of keeping yourself in front of the press and the public, always in the best possible taste of course. And just hanging on in there, sometimes by your fingernails.

At your very first success in New York, did you feel that this was it, you had arrived and that you were going to be on the top forever, so that when you came down to earth with a bump, it was all the more dramatic?

No, I think my feelings were, 'What am I doing here?' I suffer from a distinct lack of confidence in what I do, I always have.

Is that a driving factor?

I think so, because it does make you try that little bit harder. You look at other people's work and you think, 'Oh goodness that's so good, why didn't I think of that?' But then you have to look at yourself and think, 'Well I did something like that,' or, 'What I've just done is just as nice.' All the time, you're questioning.

What did it teach you when you came down to earth with a bump the first time?

When I arrived in New York, I had gone first-class, and was picked up by a limousine, taken to the Plaza, where I stayed for about a week; it was very, very glamorous. A few months later, I was going back to JFK on a Greyhound bus.

It was as bad as that?

It was.

Why did it go wrong?

Well, I was just a young kid straight out of college. I knew nothing about commerce, I knew nothing about really putting a collection together, and really that should have been their job not mine – I just designed the stuff, they were supposed to market it and make it into a saleable range of products. I remember quite distinctly, the president of the store, a very clever woman, coming into my office saying, 'That's wonderful, blah, blah, blah,' and I said, 'Will it sell?' Even at that point I was aware of commerciality and the fact that if you didn't sell, then you were on a hiding to nothing. I was quite confused because I knew things had to sell, but I knew also that there was an onus upon me to create something that was different, and that I think is the problem with fashion – because it happens twice a year, it's quite a drain and a strain on one's nerves.

So I don't know what it did teach me, really. It taught me not to rely too heavily on the press - I got good press – and that usually you find (it's been borne out time and time again) that if the press like the collection, it won't sell.

Really? You would go as far as that?

It's pretty much the case. We've seen it so many times where the press have said, 'Fantastic!' perhaps because one's played a bit to the gallery and there's not enough commercial sense there. It's quite interesting: people say that the English fashion industry produces creative people, but the businesses don't go anywhere.

The reason for this is because, if you look at the French runways and the Italian runways, they put the most crazy things on the runway just to grab media attention and it works, but if you go backstage or to the showrooms, there you have the most basic commercial goods. Whereas what happens in England is that young designers come up, and put up all the eye-catching creations for the press, but that is actually all they've got. They haven't got the commercial stuff in the back, so of course the businesses go nowhere.

So the really successful fashion designer has to have one or two products that are going to grab press attention, but beneath that there has to be a core of products that people actually want to buy and wear for almost everyday use?

Yes, that's exactly right. I do wish a few other pundits had realized this about 20 years ago. They could have taught me a few things.

And is it a mistake that a lot of young fashion designers make, going for the headline-grabbing outfits and ignoring their core?

Well, I think it is generally at this date, but now two English fashion designers are proving me wrong. One, having worked for Givenchy for the last two or three seasons is now being given the top job in Paris at Dior, and another has just taken his place at Givenchy.

If praise from the media isn't a factor, how do you sell a collection? What are the factors that persuade people to buy your work?

That's very difficult. There is a school of thought at the moment that editorial means very, very little, that it is advertising that sells. It used to be that people didn't respect advertising too much, but they felt that having editorial pages, being chosen by the fashion editors was far more influential on the consumer than advertising. But now the advertising pages are so good. Firms such as Gucci and Armani produce in their ads the dream that they want to spin, and I think the consumer finds it far more credible than the editorial.

Is that dream about the actual outfits, or is it something removed from them?

Well, take Ralph Lauren: he's a perfect example of creating a whole mood, he's selling a whole concept of life, a way of living, a lifestyle.

Does that worry you?

Well no, because every business relies on selling more than once. If you only sell to a consumer once, then fine, you may have a good season, but actually you want to have two, three or four good seasons, and to achieve that the consumer has to go back. There has to be a modicum of value in the product otherwise they won't go back. The product has to have integrity otherwise the customer just doesn't go back, and if he doesn't go back, then you're lost.

Are you ever slightly amazed, do you sit back and wonder about the extent of your success?

Never.

You don't think 'Wow, how come I'm here, that I've made this, that I've done that'?

I actually don't, but something odd might happen to prompt it. For instance, I was in the royal palace in Jordan and His Majesty walked into the room and said, 'Bruce, I saw you on television in Pakistan the other day.' That's strange, it's odd to think that King Hussein should make the connection with this guy who's dressing his daughter-in-law to the guy he saw last week on television, but I don't spend any thinking time on it.

Success doesn't really come overnight, it's always a series of steps that you make and at each step you arrive, you say, 'OK that's done, next step, that's done, next step...' It's a cumulative thing, so it's only on occasions where for example, you get an OBE, and you go to the Palace that you think, 'That's special.' So there are special times when you think, 'Well, I haven't done badly really,' but it's not something you spend a lot of time thinking about.

So perhaps a really successful person never feels that they have actually made it because there's always a hunger to move on to the next step?

Yes exactly. I've got so much going on at the moment that I'm totally over-stressed. I think I have learned to delegate in the last few years, but only because, say, six years ago, things were so horrendous. That's when I learned to type, because I didn't even have a secretary. My computer skills are handy now.

A lot of people would find that strange, someone as successful as you not having a secretary.

Well we just had to cut back. Six years ago I completely changed track – I didn't become a bus driver, but I had a business which was bulky and mismanaged which I basically got rid of. I almost restarted, and that was at the beginning of the recession and I did get back to being almost an executive. I was doing everything, which was good because I really got control of things again.

To what extent do you think your success has been a product of your background and upbringing?

I think it's probably got a lot to do with my background. I was brought up by a woman who was a dressmaker, so it was almost inevitable.

Do you think it was her imposing her ideas on you, or were you separately, for other reasons, deciding at that early stage, that you wanted to be a fashion designer?

I don't think it was her and I don't think either of us made a conscious decision because her expectations for us children were quite low. Our career expectations were very, very low.

Why?

I don't know. We're talking about the 1950s, up in County Durham, a very working-class environment. We were very poor, seven of us living in a two-up two-down, with a loo in the back – it wasn't even a flush loo. It really was quite primitive; but she did try very hard.

And she was your foster-mother? You were sent to Barnardo's when you were one-and-a-half days old. Did that have an effect on your life, looking back?

What you've never had you don't really know about. I have foster-brothers and foster-sisters and half of us would say it did have a deleterious effect, the other half would disagree, but I think you either make something or you moan about it for the rest of your life.

Feeling sorry for yourself is a total waste of time, you just have to get on with it. But by the same token, I don't actually say to myself, 'Think positively about your background, just take it in your stride.' It's not a conscious thought.

Was there a foster-father?

No, there was no father, so there was a single woman bringing up boys.

Were you all adopted?

We were all fostered, we weren't adopted. There's a difference. There are a few things that I always find slightly irritating and slightly unsettling. The fact that we were fostered and not adopted meant that she was being paid – now we know that she wasn't being paid very much, but nevertheless she was being paid – there was always a feeling of, 'What value did the system put on us?'

The other thing was that there was always a threat of being sent back to the home. Now I don't think children in normal families have parents with any recourse to send them away. I don't know what the equivalent punishment would be. So there was always that. And I remember it was that you could get sent back to the home, and then, when I was back in Barnardo's, they would say, 'You'll end in Borstal,' or, 'You'll be made a ward of court.' There was always such threats.

Were you a trouble-maker?

I was dreadful, yes. It was just that they expected so little and I expected so much. I wasn't going to drop down to their level, I was going to maintain my level, so there was always remarks like, 'Who do you think you are and why do you think you're any different from the rest?' And those negative forces, I think, always made me rebel.

And they didn't pull you down at any stage?

Oh, I wanted to react against them and I did; and it is funny, actually, because when I left Spennymoor, County Durham, and went to Ripon, I was put into quite a different environment, into a Barnardo's Home with 24 boys and having passed my 11+, I went to the local grammar school.

I was the only one at the local grammar school – even the superintendent's son didn't go there, much to his annoyance. This is why he didn't get on very well with me, this is why he was always saying, 'Who do you think you are?'

So there was kind of resentment amongst some of the others that you were going to this grammar school?

Oh yes, and also there's a classic resentment because the grammar school's opposite, the secondary modern school, didn't wear uniforms and we did, so we were the snobby grammar school twits and they – well, I can't remember what we called them!

You always had a deep inner confidence about your abilities?

Yes, and I think it manifested itself at quite an early age, because I seem to remember people saying, 'Who do you think you are?' from quite an early age.

During your schooldays you had a stutter – now why should someone who was so confident have a stutter?

A stutter is more of a physical thing, it's not being able to get your words out fast enough. I think you can be confident in your abilities and still be nervous.

How long did it take you to get over those nerves?

Oh, I still have them, I stuttered until I was about 19 or 20. It was terrible, it really was, and the problem with a stutter is that you spend a lot of time worrying about it and when you have to read in class, in French, in Latin or in German or English, whatever it happened to be, I would work out which passage I would have judging by how many paragraphs the teacher was asking each person to do, so I would be right ahead, not taking any notice what was going on, just practising my entry into my paragraph – sometimes I got it, sometimes I didn't. I spent so much time at school wasting time doing that.

Going back to your schooldays, did you resent authority?

I really hated Spennymoor Grammar School with a passion. I was unhappy with my foster mother; things weren't going very well there. When I was sent to Ripon, Ripon Grammar School was a completely different environment. In fact it was the best thing that ever happened to me. And I don't think I did rebel against authority there because I thought that it was fair. It was a very liberal grammar school, whereas Spennymoor was more focused on boys going out into industry.

So when they criticized you at Ripon you thought, 'They've got a point'?

Yes, and it was usually more fairly put.

Tell me the story about being asked to cut the grass with scissors.

Well, I was never very good at games. (Though now I love going to the gym. I run for an hour, three times a week, at about 6.30 in the morning.) Anyway, I was never very keen on games, so this particular time, I probably had provoked a teacher at Ripon School slightly, by turning up without my kit. It was the summer, and this particular teacher I had never got on with. 'OK,' he said, 'You can cut the grass around the tennis courts with these shears.' 'Oh sod this,' I thought. I threw the shears on the floor and walked out, walked off, left.

Left the school?

Left the school. So I went back to Barnardo's, and said to the superintendent, 'I think I've been rather stupid,' and he said, 'Well, that's your fault, tough.' This was a Friday, so Monday morning I was dreading the repercussions.

After assembly, the head master said, 'Could I see Oldfield in my office straight after assembly.' I didn't know what he was going to do, but he said, 'Two things Bruce. One, don't ever throw scissors at my staff, and two, don't ever leave school without permission. Off you go.' Which I thought was fair because what he was basically saying was that he thought that that member of staff was probably being a little bit overbearing and he was also covering himself since he was responsible for us between the hours of nine and four. So I thought it was fair.

You may think that I was pushing my luck and that I should have been whipped around the goalpost, but to me he was fairer than the superintendent of Barnardo's who, I thought, was just cavalier and dismissive.

But he helped maintain your respect for the institution of school?

Indeed, and I don't think I ever did it again.

Did you have a mentor, someone at school who ran along side you, who rode shotgun to your life, as it were?

I didn't really.

Have you had mentors in your life?

I have had a few, usually they're women. There was the head mistress of Ripon Grammar School, who took me slightly under her wing. When I only got two A-levels, which meant I couldn't get into university, she said, 'Apply to teacher training college.' I didn't think I wanted to go to teacher training college, but anyway I applied there and I got in.

You'd abandoned your earlier ambition to be a fashion designer?

Well no, my early ambition to be a fashion designer was never really followed up because, one, it was not the kind of career for a boy, absolutely not, and then of course I was told, 'Get your qualifications, get your O-levels, get your A-levels, then get a degree.' Something to fall back on; everybody's looking for safety nets.

Do you think it stops a lot of people pursuing the career they want to go for from an early age when people say, 'Get your qualifications – something to fall back on'?

Absolutely. And the funniest thing is, I was speaking to some kids from Cambridge University the other day, because they want me to do something next year, and one of the girls said, 'Well, I'm studying law but I've no intention of being a lawyer,' and I thought, 'This sounds exactly like, "Well I'm studying to be a teacher but I've no intention of being a teacher."'

I think that if you have the possibility at the age of 18 to go on for higher education, certainly in my day, then you would do it, you wouldn't choose to go to work if you had the opportunity to be a student. I don't know whether it's the same today, but I did think that people do get a bit bogged down by their parents' notions, or by the perceived wisdom of 'you need to have a qualification'.

I mean, I did not have any qualifications in the end. I completed a three-year course in teacher training, but I didn't do the one-year's teaching which you have to do to get the proper diploma: I didn't finish at arts school; I did one year at Ravensbourne and one year at St Martin's and I left in the second year – to great rapturous applause.

Because by that time you had already established yourself?

Well, by that time I had been a student for five years; I was 23 and I was sick of it and I had won the Sarga Mink competition, which is the fur competition, which practically every student in fashion in the country did; then I was the overall winner in 1973, then part of this promotion for the launch of Charlie (a Revlon perfume back in the 1970s) and for that, I had to put together a collection, myself and a girl called Paulene Mucha from St Martin's. We were asked to do six designs each.

That was all in that second year at St Martin's and so when it got to June I just thought – and I'd had so much press – I thought, 'Why not leave? They aren't teaching me very much.' I felt I could learn much more by being out and one month later, Geraldine Stutz, the President of Bendels arrived in my street in Brixton in a huge white limo and this doyenne of New York fashion came up the stairs, curled up on the chair and murmured sweet nothings in my ears, and, of course, I said 'Yes.' Also I was making clothes for Bianca Jagger so I was down there on Cheyne Walk in Chelsea with Mick Jagger and Ryan O'Neal running in and out and Marissa Berenson, I was thinking, 'Hey, I like this!'

Did it go to your head?

Of course it went to my head. It went totally to my head, I was probably the most arrogant pratt known to man. But the New York experience did bring me slightly back down to earth. Although I don't think it necessarily dented my total confidence, it probably scratched the surface a bit. But it didn't do any serious damage. I think it just makes you stronger, makes you think, 'I'll show you.'

And then you had this marvellous progression until you hit the rock of the recession at the end of the 1980s. What went wrong there?

What went wrong was that we, as a company, were always under-capitalized, rather like all the young designers – they leave college and start a business without a business partner, without proper finance, and so on. A business, like fashion, needs to be properly marketed: you do need an advertising budget; you do need to be able to put on shows using proper models; you need a lot of investment; and in England, fashion is not considered to be a very serious game.

If you want to appeal to the lowest common denominator and hit the high street then, yeah, you can do it, but if you want to do anything where quality is a major part of it, of both design and product, then you've got to console yourself with the fact that you are always going to remain very small. You either make one-offs for individual clients, sell to department stores or open your own retail outlet, those are the three things that you do.

All of these separate moves cost a lot of money and it's where the investment is required. We found some investors through the Business Expansion Scheme in the early 1980s which enabled us to open the first shop in Beauchamp Place, which has always made money. But in order to make the name bigger it was necessary to do wholesale and to sell to other stores, broadening your base, but also requiring more money.

If you're doing the Winter 1997 collection, for instance, you order the sample fabrics in October 1996, make the samples by the end of January 1997, present them to the stores in March, produce the goods and deliver them in July and get paid – if you're lucky! – in September–October. That's quite an investment in time and money with no income, only outlay!

So you rely on sales and good turnover to fund that?

Yes, and once you start making a lot of clothes, then you can start making money if, like any business, you keep a very tight control on it and watch it. The other way of expanding your business is to go into licensing, which is what all the Americans do, where you find a partner who will produce things under your name for you and market them and sell them on to the shops. But they must do it in a way which is consistent with your reputation, your name and your standing and the quality that you are known for.

That's when it all falls to pieces. In the mid to late 1980s I had a lot of licensing deals – shoes, tights, furs, glasses, jewellery, shirts, endless things – and in a way what we were trying to do was to build the core of Bruce Oldfield product, every label said 'Bruce Oldfield for somebody'. The companies that we were dealing with weren't big enough or competent enough really to run the course, so when it got to 1989–90, everybody was feeling the pinch and a lot of those companies suddenly thought, 'Hey, our core business is suffering here, let's get back to it, get rid of all these licensees.'

So how close did you come to disaster, to bankruptcy?

How close? I had a meeting with all of my good lawyers and accountants and partners, because I had partners and they were saying, 'Basically, we think it's time to just pull the plug,' and I said, 'No.' I'm not trying to sound like a martyr, but I did feel, that I'd just been given my OBE and it says on this document, 'To our trusted and well beloved Bruce Oldfield.' 'Well,' I thought, 'it wouldn't be thought trusting and well-beloved to go bankrupt.'

Quite often bankruptcy is used as a simple device to get out of trouble when you know, if you really dug your heels in you could actually trade out of it. So I said, 'No, no can do.'

What steps did you take to actually save the business?

I just closed everything. We had offices in Fulham, a big place which I was paying a reverse premium to get out of for three years. I just retrenched so tightly and I sold my flat and I moved to Battersea, that's not such a big deal but never mind. There was a psychological thing about moving from SW3 to SW11 you know, especially when you're on the river bank and you're looking at SW3 longingly for three years. I finally got back. I just got rid of everybody that I didn't need.

We got rid of all of the things that were just draining the company. It was very, very hard to come back to just doing couture again, which is what I did.

So what you're saying is that as you became more and more successful and the company expanded and the staff grew, in a sense you took your eye off the financial war, is that right?

I think I took an eye off the financial war and also off the core business, the part of the business that had always been most successful, which was the couture and the limited ready-to-wear that we did through Beauchamp Place. That was always what was successful, it was doing all of those other things that caused the core, the real business, to take second place.

Is it true that the more you charge in fashion, the more successful you are seen to be?

Everyone is always saying that couture is dead, but I find that the couture side of the business is the most profitable; it's the one that's growing. Throughout the recession the turnover and the profitability of this company rose 20 per cent per year. I was continually raising my standards and therefore my prices, but it just didn't seem to matter – people were still buying it.

This season, I've got quite a lot of things that are up in the £7–8,000 range which we sell 10 or 12 of per piece – that's a lot of the business on one frock. And here at Beauchamp Place, we can do £34,000 in a day without really having to work terribly hard and over at Brook Street, if we do £34,000 in a week, we're jumping up and down.

So why move into ready-to-wear?

Well, I finally got to the point where I wasn't challenged enough – this was about a year and a half ago – so I sat down and I decided on a plan to expand the business again because it was time; my business was solid because the company was profitable again. I didn't want to be just a little couturier for the rest of my life; it's very nice but I need more challenges than that. I need to be out there, I need to be doing things.

So it seemed obvious that I'd got to get back into ready-to-wear, but I only wanted to do it through my own retail outlet. This was the business plan that I put together, and I found two partners that were very keen to go with it, but what I did was grant the licence to them. You see, I own this business completely, 100 per cent, and I own all the trademarks and all the copyrights completely; all I do is I licence it out.

So the way you're making money now – apart from the couture business which is your own – is to license your name and your reputation to others?

Yes, and keep full control, unlike in the 1980s when we were licensing the name to a company to manufacture something. I'm not doing that at all. What I am doing is I've started this business which is like a joint venture, because I'm part of a business, I have a stake in that particular business – the ready-to-wear business – but I also license my name to that particular business and I am paid by that business and I get a royalty from that business, but I could withdraw my name from it. It's a very, very strict retailing concept.

But you've cracked the funding now because it's your partners who are putting up the money?

Yes, my partners put up the money. To show good faith I have also put in some money myself.

So where it is possible, one of the secrets is to get other people to put up as much of the money as possible?

Yes, but you have to guide them, because they will all say to you, 'You must come up with the concepts for this, that and the other,' which is fine.

So how much control do you exert?

I exert a lot of control, and I have to. At the moment the operation is quite small because I've got Beauchamp Place and I've got Brook Street.

As you expand and as you develop, are you going to have to delegate more?

Yes, I'm going to have to rely on the partners in the joint ventures that we set up overseas because I can't be there and in Melbourne, where the next shop is about to open, for example; it's difficult enough to be in Beauchamp Place and in Brook Street.

So is the potential there for things to go wrong because you are not holding the reigns as fully as you have been used to in the past?

There's always a potential for things to go wrong, but because these people are putting in all of the money, they're going to be watching their investment as well. This is the secret too: you have to make sure that they are going by the standards which you've set and that they always maintain those standards.

That's always the danger in our business – allowing standards to slip. I walk into Brook Street and if there's a thread hanging from a dress or if there's smut on the carpet... I will actually pick up dog-ends outside the shop in full view of the staff, just so that they see me doing it, and go in with them in my hand and say, 'Can we get rid of these please?' The next day you go, there are no dog-ends, probably a week later the dog-ends are back, so you've got to do it again, and that is the problem – people are sloppy.

And don't learn?

They don't learn, they don't take an interest because it's not theirs. That's why with partners for the venture abroad, hopefully they will see that it's theirs and that it is encumbent upon them to maintain standards.

So success lies in paying attention to the detail?

Absolutely. Not only the business detail, in my business it's also the visual detail, because that's the thing the customer sees first. If you're in, say, nuts and bolts, then the problem is slightly different; in fashion you have to be careful that your threads are correct.

We're talking about attention to detail in all kinds of ways. You aren't a little pernickety in devoting so much time to detail?

It's not only the visual thing. For instance, I constantly get detailed analysis about how things are selling, size ratios that are selling. We may find that we are not selling trousers and you think, 'Why?' The answer is that people are coming purely for special-occasion things and on a special occasion they don't think they can wear trousers. So cut down the trousers for the next season – we have to have some because it is a trouser season and the press will want trousers – but base most of it on skirts; it is that kind of detail. You do have managers for that, but then you have to hand pick the managers. At the moment Brook Street is running managerless – I am the manager.

Have you ever felt like giving up?

No. I haven't got anything else that I'm dying to do.

No frustrated ambitions?

No, people say, 'You could do interiors.' Yes I could, but then I probably will do interiors as part of the whole thing. I'll do the interiors of the shops and perhaps there will be a home product line at some point. I think I can get so much from the business that I have, so I don't really see what else I would do.

Does luck play a part in success?

I don't believe in luck. Luck is something that you can manipulate, I don't think it's something that just happens. People say, 'You're so lucky!' and I say, 'Yes you can make your luck, you can position yourself.' There probably is an element of luck somewhere, but it's mainly you manoeuvring yourself into a situation where luck happens just to be.

Who are the people whose success you really admire, either past or present, in your profession or outside it?

I have become very, very cynical because I know the story behind so much of where other fashion designers are, I know the public perception and I know the truth of it. But a person I admire very much is Georgio Armani and I admire him for his good taste. I admire Karl Largerfeld, he's a very good designer, and he's very astute, he doesn't have his own line as such, he just works with other people. He calls himself a mercenary which is quite right. He makes a fortune.

Is there a great contrast between the reality and the impression that people give?

Yes, of course.

Are you driven by money?

I have really never been driven by money. Somebody read my hand the other day – it was a client – and she said, 'You must be very, very careful about somebody looking after your money, I see something very funny here.' I'm not money-driven, I don't know what drives me. Actually, I want to succeed; I want to be Georgio Armani, really.

Are you after a level of respect from your peers or from the public?

I think it's both of those things and a financial stability. I think it's recognition and stability.

You are stable now, why go on and want more?

It's probably because I haven't got anything else to do. I haven't got a wife, child, or lover, so I might as well get on. I wake up early in the morning, so I'm quite happy to speak to Sydney or Melbourne or Tokyo, it's no skin off my nose. I'm happy when I'm engaged in this, the cut-and-thrust of it, thinking about it. I like the business side and I like chasing something and getting it.

And work is your life then, your total life?

Yes, sad isn't it?

Do you think it's sad?

I think it's a little sad, yes, but I think that we all have capacity for certain things. I have the capacity to tirelessly bang on and on about developing my business and I don't feel that

I'm missing out on anything else, particularly.

Is it becoming more or less difficult to achieve success in your particular field?

I think that now, opportunities for me are arising on an almost daily basis, certainly since opening the boutique. The opportunities that come in from all parts of the world are quite staggering because I've suddenly repositioned myself and said, 'OK, yes I do couture but I also manufacture very nice clothes for a wider audience, what do you think and any ideas?' And they seem to be coming.

What do you think are the greatest enemies of success?

Jealousy, over-reaching yourself, over-reaching your capabilities. I think the English press don't help.

In what way are they unhelpful?

The English press are very negative about success, they encourage it to be given, then they sort of say, 'He's getting a bit cocky, we'll have to sort him out.'

Why do you think they do that?

I think it's that puritanical, English streak. It's quite funny actually now Britain is so much more entrepreneurial since the 1980s. Entrepreneurialism is not a dirty word; I think it was.

But do you feel the press goes further than just keeping people on their toes in a healthy sort of way?

Yes. The press can be very vindictive when they want to be. Touch wood, they have never been to me particularly, I've always had a reasonable press. I find that if you over-expose, you start to see them turn; there's a sting in the tail.

So the important factor in success is judging when to push and promote yourself, your ideas, your products, and when to pull up the drawbridge?

Yes, and sometimes you have to pull it up really fast, if you see the signs. I saw the signs earlier this year, when there were two or three pieces that came out where I was mentioned in not a particularly favourable light, and that was when I said, 'OK, stop.'

Has success changed you at all?

I don't think it has, actually. It's nice and it's not nice; it's nice when you can get a good seat in a restaurant and get upgraded on a plane, but it's slightly difficult when you're walking down the street or you're in Harrods Food Hall or wherever it is and somebody thinks that they can come and have a chat. You tend to have to go around with a fixed smile on your face because otherwise the next thing you hear two days later, is that somebody said they saw you down the street and you totally ignored them.

What is the greatest pleasure you've had from your success?

Independence. Getting the OBE was a recognition that I was OK at what I did, that I'd got there, that I'd done something. For that reason I do like getting awards.

If you could gather together before you in one room all the budding fashion designers at technical college or preparing to go to university to study fashion, bearing in mind all the present circumstances and difficulties that exist within your profession, what advice would you give them to give them a reasonable chance of being as successful as Bruce Oldfield has become?

A lot of things – don't believe in your own publicity. Go and work for somebody else and learn about the business side of the industry. Please don't start on your own unless you've got someone with some business acumen and finance behind you. I think those are the two most important things. Another very good piece of advice is don't get too involved; there are so many new, fresh designers coming up all the time.

And as you move up the ladder, what are the core ingredients of a successful fashion business?

Being correctly financed because it does cost a lot of money. Not only are you manufacturing, you've got to put yourself out, you've got to maintain an image to the public through public relations, advertising, marketing and fashion shows. If you want to produce perfect things in this country, stay small.

You're not doing that?

But you see I am because I am keeping hold of this business, the core business, which is my couture business; that's where I'll always be found. The other part is delegation.

When your time comes to depart this life, what would you like people to say about you?

Something along the lines of, 'He tried hard.' That could mean one of two things: he tried hard but he didn't do that well; or, he tried hard and didn't he do well and look what happens when you try hard. It's a nice open-ended, ambiguous epitaph, don't you think?

LORD SAATCHI

'There is a point,' says Maurice Saatchi, 'at which a child decides itself that it wants to succeed for its own reasons. Parents cannot make that click in the head happen.' For the man who, with his brother Charles, ran the first British company to get to the top of world advertising, that 'click' clearly happened early.

One of four sons of a prosperous Jewish textile merchant who brought his young family to Britain from Iraq in 1946, he worked in 'an obsessive fashion' to obtain good marks at school and university. His analytical skills earned him a first-class degree from the London School of Economics. To his professor's disappointment, he opted for a career in business instead of research, launching Saatchi & Saatchi with Charles at the age of 24. He once described their business as 'more than a company – it's an attitude'.

By 1986, they had 5 per cent of the world's advertising, with a host of major clients such as British Airways and Mars. But in 1994, moving steadily along the takeover trail – and even eyeing up the Midland Bank – they over-reached themselves.

He now puts the blame for that on 'a sense of arrogance' which led him to decline 'good advice from sensible people'. But within days, he had created a new company, M & C Saatchi, 'on a tide of strong emotion among employees and clients, the like of which I'd never seen before'.

Here he opens up in more detail than ever before about the thinking and the influences that have shaped his remarkable career. He talks about the difference between selling products and political ideas. Married to the Irish novelist Josephine Hart, he finds the opening words of her first book compelling: 'Damaged people are dangerous. They know they can survive.' But he tempers that with President Truman's comment that 'being bitter is for people who don't have something else to do.'

Lord Saatchi, what is your definition of success?

To make a ripple in the pond.

How big a ripple do you think you've made?

That's for others to say.

Why is it important to make a ripple?

It's an expression of an individual contribution.

Do you see it as a contribution to the economy, to society, or to what?

I don't think it makes very much difference what the field of endeavour happens to be. If you want to make a ripple there's only one way to do it, and that is to try to be the best there is in your chosen sphere, whether it is art or sport or politics or business. It only happens if you aim to be the best in your particular speciality.

So being the best ought to be a target for everyone who wants to be successful? It shouldn't be something that happens to you almost by accident – it should be a specific goal?

Yes. That is the only route I know to success in any field.

To what extent do you think your success is due to your background and your upbringing?

Freud attributes most of the misfortune or success of an adult life to early upbringing and the relationship between the child and the parents. So I think that is fundamental.

What was the nature of the relationship between you and your parents?

Your father came over from Iraq in 1946 and set up home in North London. What kind of an upbringing did you and your brothers have?

It was orientated to hard work and doing the best you could. It's very striking – and I notice it now with my own children – that there is a point at which a child decides itself that it wants to succeed for its own reasons, for its own pride.

Not every child comes to that point, but I imagine that the children who go on to be successful in later life have experienced a moment when it becomes important *to them* to do well. And that, surely, is a critical turning point in every person's life.

To be successful in whatever is your chosen sphere, you must see a point B, know yourself to be at point A, and believe that you would be happier if you moved to point B. I think it goes on from there for the rest of your life.

Can your parents shepherd you on to that path, or is it a path you have to decide to reach yourself, at whatever age you decide to jump on to it?

I can only speak as a son and a father. My observation, in both roles, would be that it's a decision which an individual makes or doesn't make for himself, and that parents cannot make that click in your head happen for their child.

But can they help by creating the right environment?

There is no 'right' environment. I don't see that there's any particular merit or virtue in either of the two approaches. It's not necessary to have that linear A to B approach to achieve happiness in life. The people who decide to take that route believe they can see a point B where, they believe, they will be happy. But it's not necessarily an objective fact, and it's not necessarily the way to happiness for all people, or even most people.

For example, Milan Kundera described happiness as a circle. He said it was a mistake to have a linear approach and to strive to reach point B. For him, happiness is the endless circular repetition of pleasurable acts, rather than something directional. So there are many ways to achieve happiness.

Do you think that happiness and success go hand in hand?

They are the same thing. Success *is* the achievement of happiness.

Just take me through your days at school, your qualifications, and going on to the London School of Economics, what you achieved there.

I was an intense schoolboy, always interested in achieving good grades. And I worked, I would say, in an obsessive fashion to earn those results at school and a good degree at university. I took it rather seriously.

After LSE you went to work for the Haymarket Group as business development manager, to the great disappointment of your professor at university, who thought that you were poised to go into research?

Yes, well, my tutor, was a generous man. He was kind enough to say that I could have gone on to pursue an academic life.

So why didn't you?

Ironically, because the LSE was so inspiring. I enjoyed the economics course so much – the main specialization was in sociology and social psychology – that I wanted to apply what I'd learned. Of course, I didn't work all this out in the rational way I'm describing now.

So you then saw that you could apply that in business, though not necessarily, at that stage, in advertising?

No, at that stage advertising hadn't come into my life at all. It had just been a part of what I had studied, so I was interested in all forms of communication. I didn't know quite why, but I was fascinated by it, and I now realize that it was the result of the teaching I had at LSE.

I spent two or three years with Haymarket, and I was given a very grand title for which I was grateful. I had a sort of cupboard as an office, and the job I had was to try to define new magazine launches or acquisitions which the company could make, and to pursue them, which we did vigorously. I enjoyed it immensely because I was working for people I admired.

But then you decided to switch to advertising. What was the catalyst for that?

Charles, who had been a great success in advertising at that time.

That was with the campaign of the pregnant man?

Yes. We discussed the possibility of starting an advertising agency ourselves. He had his perspective on the advertising world; I had a completely different perspective, from the point of view of a media owner, where you come into contact with advertising agencies from a different angle. I felt sure there were all sorts of things that could be done better, as sure as only somebody of 24 could feel. So we agreed to have a go.

Were you a bit nervous about setting out on your own at the age of 24, and giving up a good job and what must have been a certain amount of financial security to do so?

Yes, I was. And also sad to leave Haymarket, where I had been very happy.

At what point did you begin to think, 'This is clicking, this is really going to work, it's really taking off as an advertising company. It's something in which I'm going to spend my life'?

I think that took about six months. The fear of failure – which, of course, besets every new business as an ever-present threat – ended after only about six months, because the company was profitable from then on.

How did you achieve that? Was there an element of luck to it, or was it all good planning?

It was huge good luck. We won some great clients. So we were paying our way as a new company, and we never really looked back.

But you were moving into an established market in which there were some very big names and you were, if you like, the cheeky upstart, the newcomer. That's quite a daunting prospect. A lot of people might have decided that it wasn't worth taking the risk. What drove you to take that risk?

Soon after the company was set up – alarmingly soon, for many people, I would say – we decided that the company wasn't going to collapse and that we could do well. We had a touching degree of faith in the wisdom of what we were trying to do, and in the merits of it. So it had the feeling of a crusade.

The crusade was a simple one, which was an important factor. As we saw the advertising industry at that time, clients faced a choice between small, probably very bright and creative young agencies on the one hand, and on the other, big, multi-national giants who were more reliable and disciplined and safe as suppliers of advertising, but who perhaps lacked the creative sparkle of the smaller and younger companies. So our purpose was to try to achieve the impossible – to have a big agency which would provide the stability that was important to both clients and employees, but somehow to combine size with being dynamic, youthful and innovative.

We had a phrase for this. It was: 'It's good to be big, it's better to be good, but it's best to be both.' And we really worked at that: it was our credo throughout the company's history literally from that point, about six months after the foundation of the agency.

And what did you and your brother specifically bring to the table? Did you complement each other? Were you bringing specific clear skills, or were you both spreading your energy and enthusiasm around all areas?

We were completely different. Charles was the creative one – he actually wrote advertisements and had ideas, and that, of course, is the only skill that matters in advertising. I was what is known as the 'suit', the one who carries the bag. Advertising agencies, basically, are composed of those two talents, of which the former is far more important.

A great many people, when they start off on their own, have some kind of mentor or mentors behind them. Did you have anyone like that, and do you think that every successful person, at some stage in their life, needs a mentor?

Everyone needs a hero.

Is there a difference?

Only in the sense that a mentor would be somebody you know personally and to whom you can talk. Whereas a hero could be anyone, alive or dead, who is your role model.

Certainly, I had heroes in advertising. I think probably the greatest was Bill Bernbach, who was the founder of an agency called Doyle Dane Bernbach. He had a particular approach to advertising which was based on creativity, and he changed the face of the industry. Prior to his arrival on the scene, advertising had been based very much on the concept of sheer salesmanship, of the doorstep variety: a hard, rational sell.

Bernbach's idea was that when the salesman calls at the door, it helps him to make the sale if you, the customer, actually *like* him. If you like him, you're more likely to like his product. This, of course, sounds quite straightforward now, but at the time, in the 1960s, it was a revolutionary concept. It led to the more emotional and image-based advertising that now probably accounts for the bulk of the industry's output around the world. He did that.

As the agency developed, did you have any maxims for what made a good advertising agency? I'm thinking of statements like, 'Keep a tidy desk and phone the client every day.' Is that accurate?

I don't think we had maxims like that. But there was a powerful ethos and a strong, shared sense of culture in the company which made it special. And I think it came from the original drive to achieve what, on the face of it, was impossible: namely, that elusive combination of size and creativity.

How important were people to the organization? It's a popular view that, in the world of advertising, people are really the only asset you've got.

There is nothing else in an advertising agency, so that proverb about the assets going up and down in the lift is true. It's true of all specialized service companies. And the people we had in the company were the best in the industry, as it later turned out.

How did you pick them? How did you identify their qualities? What were you looking for when you put the team together?

Several of them were there right at the beginning, and others came in the early years, the first five years, and stayed for many years thereafter. In terms of qualities, I don't think I can lay enough stress on that sense of purpose, of knowing why you were going to work and what you were trying to achieve, and the feeling that if you did achieve that, it would be very special. The knowledge that they were serving some greater goal was inspiring to people.

The process of finding the right people was by self-selection. Because the company did stand for something specific, and if you stand for something you will divide people. There will be those who are for you and others who are against you, so those who came into the company were the people who wanted to be a part of that crusade.

I think you have said that Saatchi's is more than a company, it's an attitude. Is loyalty an important part of that?

Loyalty to that concept, faith in that concept, I would regard as fundamental.

What makes a successful advertisement and a successful advertising campaign? Are there any clear core ingredients which they all must have?

Yes. Bertrand Russell, talking about happiness and how to achieve it, said that it requires 'the painful necessity of thought'. The advertisements which work are those which have been thought through with great precision, and which are not vague and do not confuse the simple message they are trying to deliver. So deep thought, leading to simplicity of expression.

How much thought will go into creating a great five-word buzz phrase used by a company to sell a product?

Winston Churchill once wrote a letter to a friend which began: 'I wanted to write you a short letter, but I didn't have time.' That explains what I mean. To achieve simplicity, the short phrase you mentioned, requires much greater effort than a long and rambling sentence. Anyone can do that. These days audiences around the world are so sophisticated, so cynical, and so aware of being manipulated that only a thought through, simply expressed, distilled argument is likely to cut through the barrage of information people are receiving every day.

Does the same principle apply to political advertising as well, or are there added dimensions to a political campaign?

The political campaign bears no resemblance to product or business campaigns.

You're not selling politicians in the same way as you would sell a commercial product like soap powder?

No, I think that is a misconception. My experience of politics is that it is a world apart. It has its own laws of gravity; it has its own time zones. It is completely different from business.

Are there any generalizations you can make about a political campaign? Is it true that the best political advertising campaigns are negative?

Not necessarily. If you look back and try to think of the most effective political messages in history, you would find short phrases of great simplicity and great power. For example, '*Liberté, Egalité, Fraternité,*' or, '*Workers of the world unite, you have nothing to lose but your chains,*' or, '*I have a dream.*' These are not just slogans or soundbites, they encapsulate entire philosophies, whole political systems. Think of, '*One man, one vote,*' or, '*No taxation without representation.*' Or, '*Go West, young man.*' These are phrases which have changed the course of history. It is to that one aspires, in a humble way, in mounting political campaigns.

So for you the best kind of politician would be one who speaks in soundbites?

I do take the view that if you can't express your argument in a short, crisp, simple way it may mean there's something wrong with your argument. You see, I regard the search for simplicity as a test. It is not merely a discipline: it forces exactitude or it annihilates. To me it is the mark of a cause that is good that it can express itself in a short, powerful way.

The best example I can give you is the way President Roosevelt persuaded a profoundly isolationist America to support Britain in its' hour of greatest need. He invented a short phrase – two words – to do that: '*Lend Lease.*' And he had a simple way of expressing what that meant. He said to the American people: 'It's like this: your neighbour's house is on fire and he comes to you and asks if he can have your hose. You say to him, "I will not give you my hose, but I will lend it to you. And after you've put out your fire you will return it to me."' The American public accepted Lend Lease on that basis. So that was a moment of great importance which turned on two words.

You built up the company over 25 years. It was incredibly successful, and then everything started to go wrong with the recession. The share price plummeted and suddenly you saw your world starting to collapse. What was your approach to that situation?

The company was a marvellous company, and, by then, a very big company as well, but the recession in advertising, which brought about the first drop in world advertising expenditure since the war, arrived at a most unfortunate moment for us. We had just completed some very large acquisitions, and the timing of the recession was exquisite in its inappropriateness. But I had no doubt that the company would continue to be successful.

And yet you were losing control of the company?

We had actually lost control of the company, but I don't think at that stage we quite realized how completely. During the years of growth, we had issued a large number of shares to finance acquisitions and our shareholding in the company had been diluted from a majority controlling interest to 1 or 2 per cent. I don't think we ever foresaw the bitter harvest of that loss of control.

Looking back, was there any way that you could have foreseen it, or were you carried along on this great wave of success that made you feel that you could almost do anything, that the world was your oyster – almost a sense of arrogance?

It wasn't 'almost' a sense of arrogance – it was exactly that.

What is your judgement on what went wrong in terms of your attitude?

We had very good advice from sensible people which we declined to take.

That advice was that it was impossible to maintain what we had achieved in the previous 20 years – which was compound average growth in pre-tax profits, earnings per share and dividend per share of 32 per cent, and that beyond a certain size, it was inconceivable that we could continue to grow so much ahead of market growth.

You can probably do that when you're quite small and you have a small market share, but we were, by then, the biggest agency in the world, and our share of world advertising was quite significant. So it defied logic to think that you could grow much more than the market, but we persisted in that belief.

Why did you do that? You were defying logic; you were defying the advice of experts. You were ploughing your own furrow as you had done over the previous 25 years?

Probably a habit of defying gravity had become ingrained. We would have been much better to have said to ourselves, 'Now this is a big, mature company, and it will grow by a few percentage points more than the market, which means that perhaps it might grow by 10 per cent per annum, maybe a bit less.' That would have been a realistic, sensible goal, and we should have taken that advice.

Do you think there is a risk that every person who sets out to be successful will reach a point at which he is unable to take a realistic, objective view of his own position because it's been coloured so much by the treadmill of success he is on?

I'm certain that's the case. Don't they say that all political careers end in tears? I suppose it is true in all walks of life that it's a risk, but the alternative is to do nothing, and that's not a guaranteed route to happiness, either.

For years you didn't give interviews, and you still grant very, very few. Was it a part of your plan to create a mystique by not bowing to the normal convention of talking a lot in public about your business?

It did not begin in that way, but after a while we began to see that giving interviews was only likely to help our competitors and we didn't want to explain to the world our own view of what was making our company successful. We were sure we knew what we were doing and why, and we didn't particularly want to share that. That's how it began.

And yet wasn't part of your success the fact that so many people were writing about you?

I don't think they were writing about us because we didn't give interviews, I think they were writing about us because we did a lot of things, some of which were new, and broke new ground. There had not been a British company which had got to the top in world advertising, or anything like it.

When we first went to America, it was unheard of for a British company to acquire an American advertising agency. The industry had been completely dominated by American multi-national firms. So the idea that some British local company would come to Madison Avenue and try to buy it was considered bizarre. This sort of thing attracted quite a lot of attention.

You once said, 'Perception is reality.' Can successful advertising make people do anything, buy anything, even if deep-down they don't want to?

It depends how you define what people want. If you were to say that advertising sells people things they don't need, that would undoubtedly be true. You don't need a Hoover – you can clean a house with a broom and a dishcloth. You don't need an electric razor – you can shave with a cut-throat. So in the sense that advertising creates a demand for those kinds of innovation, it is not meeting needs, it is creating wants. But that is open to criticism only if you don't believe that the market, in trying to please the public, does so by producing better and better products and services. That's how it works.

The jury is public opinion, and companies court public opinion by offering better products and services, and the jury then decides. This, to me, adds up to advancement, but if people prefer to stay with the broom they can do so.

What do you regard as your most successful advertising campaign?

I would say the work we've done over the years for British Airways. It has been a privilege to have been involved in what is certainly one of the great business success stories for decades, probably since the war. It's been a remarkable turnaround. And if the advertising played some small part in that, I would be very pleased.

What do you regard as your biggest failure, and how did you recover from it?

It must have been to allow control of Saatchi & Saatchi to pass out of our hands – particularly into the hands of people who didn't like the advertising business at all. And how did we recover from it? We haven't.

But you have gone some way towards doing so by starting a new company. When you lost control of Saatchi & Saatchi, did you think at any stage, 'Right, well I've made my pile, I'm giving up – I don't need to go back to the beginning and start up all over again.' What was it that drove you to set up your new company?

There is a saying in politics, which is that everything is driven by events. 'Events, dear boy, events,' was how Harold Macmillan explained what shaped his life, and I can only agree.

The event of loss of control of the company was a traumatic one, but the events that followed were even more dramatic in that there was no opportunity to sit and think about alternatives. Events swept us along. It was, in fact, the only time in my life that I didn't have a point B which I knew I wanted to reach. It was a tide-in-the-affairs-of-man sensation, which I've never experienced before.

Many people in the company, some of them people I'd worked with very closely, and a lot of young people, decided that they didn't want to stay with the old company under its new owner, and a lot of clients felt the same. And so this new company was born. It was created on a tide of strong emotion among employees and clients, the like of which I'd never seen before.

Was one of those feelings revenge?

There really wasn't time for the reflective questioning of motives and aims and purposes. It all happened in a matter of weeks and it felt right, so I didn't resist.

To what do you attribute that groundswell of feeling among both employees and clients? What was special about your operation that encouraged it?

I think people were just unhappy about the turn of events.

Would you say now that you need total control to maintain success?

Our new company is a partnership in which five people are equal partners, and the key people in each of our offices in each country are also big shareholders. This is a happy state of affairs. Of course, it's one that can only be achieved in a private company. Being in the public arena has many benefits, but one of the pitfalls is loss of control. It's still a price worth paying, though, and many people pay it.

A great many people feel that to be successful in business, and in a professional career, you have to make a choice, at times, between family and work. How have you resolved that dilemma? Have you, at times, had to put your family on the back-burner in order to pursue your career?

Josephine and I devote specific time entirely to family, which is weekends. We go to Sussex and we don't see anyone. We don't entertain, and we don't go out. We have a very peaceful time.

So that's a golden rule, is it? You just have these regular islands in your life?

It's a golden rule.

Is it becoming more or less difficult to achieve success in the advertising field?

Far more difficult, I would say. When we began, the industry still operated on a local basis, and around the world in different countries, there were local agencies which were at or near the top of their industry. During the years in which we were building up Saatchi & Saatchi, the globalization of the advertising industry began. So that by the time we were the biggest agency in Britain, but had no overseas offices, we felt an endangered species.

And we were right to feel insecure because that globalization has now occurred and the advertising business is now dominated by global advertisers who are interested in co-ordinating their campaigns across countries. This is very hard to do with a disparate collection of different local agencies in individual countries.

So it's very hard to see how somebody could do quite the same today as we did. We always felt that a huge iron door was closing behind us and that we wanted to get through before it shut. I think it has now closed. So it would be much harder to achieve now what was possible through the 1970s and 1980s.

So, bearing in mind the different circumstances, what advice would you give to any young people now who are in the position you were in at Haymarket or when you were leaving the London School of Economics, whose feet are poised at the bottom of the ladder, and who really want to make as much a success of their lives, of their careers, as you have: who want to be the Maurice Saatchis of tomorrow?

The first thing I would say is that they could not pick a better industry to enter than advertising, because it is an industry based entirely on merit. There is no hierarchy, there are no gradings based on seniority or age, so young people in their early 20s can achieve top positions in advertising – something that would be considered almost impossible in any other industry. That's because it's a very open world in which the man or woman with the idea is the best person in the room. You can get ahead with brains and determination. So the first advice I'd give that person is to go have a go.

What do you think are the greatest enemies of success, the things to look out for on the way, to guard against?

Self-satisfaction, by which I mean a feeling that you've done all you can.

And what are the core qualities you need to achieve success?

The click in the head of a child. That is an act of will.

Has success changed you at all?

Only in the direction of greater humility.

A lot of people might not be able to believe that.

It is true.

So humility rather than greater confidence, or both?

Humility, because you see the world flat-on, which is a source of strength and the root of happiness.

So no rosy glows?

No, because the rosy glow fades and then you're left with reality. You may as well face it flat-on from the beginning.

Did you?

No.

So that's the best bit of advice that you could give?

I think it is, yes.

What's the single greatest pleasure you have drawn from your successful career?

My life with Josephine and our family.

Your wife, of course, is a well-known novelist. Her first novel began with the phrase: 'Damaged people are dangerous, they know they can survive.' Are damaged people more likely to succeed than those who have not had some kind of traumatic experience?

That's the hard question which Josephine's book poses. I find the phrase compelling, and it's probably the reason the book was so successful. It's clearly true, but whether that means that you must have been damaged in some way in your childhood in order to be a successful person, I don't know.

She was, I think, saying that damaged people are formidable because they have overcome the fear of failure and are therefore stronger. Whether this applies to success in the world, it's hard to say. There is a difference between survival and success.

Do you think that success brings obligations in its wake? Obligations of any kind, either to society as a whole, or to others?

Aside from the obvious obligations to society and community, there is an obligation to fulfil people's expectations; not to let people down if they have faith in you, if you've been lucky enough to win their faith. That is a profound responsibility.

Is criticism an inevitable part of success? If it is, how do you ride the attacks of critics and of those who are envious of what you've achieved?

In my own case I've been greatly helped by observing politicians and political leaders at times of great pressure.

All political leaders have periods when the weight of criticism is immense and I've learned a lesson from watching how they stand up under that kind of pressure and don't crack, don't give in. There are many admirable qualities of politicians, but that's one of the most important. It's super-human at times.

I think you have to arrive at some deeper confidence in what you're trying to achieve. Of course, people say that the only thing politicians are interested in is clinging to power. That's not my experience of politicians. I think they do have a pastoral approach, and that most politicians believe that what they're trying to do is best for the people of this country. And it's that which keeps them going under criticism.

As for envy... Harry Truman said that being bitter is for people who don't have something else to do. If you do feel envy it means you are a victim of the linear approach I described before, and have identified something you want. My best advice is go and get it.

When your time comes to leave this life, what would you like people to say about you?

I'll try to answer that with a story.

When Stanley Baldwin was Prime Minister he went to Oxford University to unveil a memorial to Scott of the Antarctic. In his speech he said an interesting thing: which was that Scott of the

Antarctic was not a success. He did not reach the South Pole first, and died, tragically, in the attempt. Baldwin said that success alone is not enough; what is enough is to have a go. And that is what I believe.

If you have a go, you're likely to lead a more interesting life, to meet more interesting people and to be a more interesting person yourself. So if I had to have a memorial I'd accept the one that Baldwin gave Scott of the Antarctic: that he had a go.

ANDREW NEIL

At the helm of the Sunday Times *through much of the 1980s and 1990s, Andrew Neil had probably the highest public profile of any British newspaper editor this century. It was a double-edged sword which helped him both to grow formidably into the job and, ultimately, to lose it.*

He hits back strongly at his critics: 'Quite often the view of others is uninformed, malicious, distorted or has its own agenda' and, even more provocatively, 'consensus opinion quite often turns out to be wrong.' This feisty Scot from a middle-class Presbyterian family attributes much of his success to the 'world-class education' he acquired at school and university in Glasgow. He was never first, but 'always up with the leaders'.

A degree in Politics and Economics took him into work for the Conservative Party, from where he was head-hunted by the Economist. *His leap to the top job at the* Sunday Times *was huge. Only 34, he had never edited a national newspaper before. He recalls: 'everybody was against me; the atmosphere was hostile and brutal; I felt if I wasn't as ruthless as they were, I would lose.'*

Now he concedes his people-management skills were not a great success. He talks too about the falling out with his boss, the media mogul Rupert Murdoch; the abortive move to present a major TV current affairs show in America ('it didn't fail — we didn't get the chance to fail'); and he develops his dramatic vision of the future world of work, and the qualities and changes of approach required to be successful. Always hunting for ways of doing things better, he complains that 'Britain is the only advanced country in the world where it seems a crime to try too hard, and where ambition is regarded as a flaw'.

Andrew Neil, what is your definition of success?

I think success is having a sense of satisfaction in whatever you're doing. You can measure success by many ways depending on what activity you're in, but in terms of success for an individual the criteria are: does it give you personal satisfaction? have you got a sense of achievement, a sense of a job well done? are you happy in your work? – given that work has become so important for most people today. At the end of the day, or week, if you can say, 'That's been a good week, I've achieved what I wanted to do, things are going well, I feel happy with myself, I have a sense of achievement within myself.' I think that is a good definition of success.

Is the judgement on whether you are successful or not dependent on your own views or is it shaped in some way by the outside world's perception of whether you have been successful or not?

It is shaped by the outside world to some extent, but the outside world can misjudge you in the short term and you can get it right in the long term. You have also got to be honest with yourself, and I think people who are successful do tend to be honest with themselves, they can be their harshest critics. If you know what you're doing it doesn't matter what the short-term judgement of the outside world is. You can live with that provided you have confidence in yourself and a clear-cut definition of what you're trying to achieve. In the long run, of course, you might hope that the outside world catches up with you and accepts that what you were trying to do has been successful.

Obviously your own view of yourself is shaped by what others are saying, but you don't want to let them influence you too much, because quite often the view of others is uninformed, malicious, distorted or has its own agenda. At the end of the day we are all subject to the judgement of the market and to our peer group and to consensus of opinion. Whether that judgement matters is itself a matter of judgement, and there are many things about which the consensus might be, 'That is a failure,' and later that consensus turns out to be wrong.

You need inner strength and confidence in your own abilities, in your own objectives, a confidence that you know what you are doing and that your critics don't, in order to know what a success is. In the longer run the two views should come together, but in the short run they might not. There's a herd instinct and a herd mentality that reinforces opinion, but you should not let other people determine what you want to do, or let their judgements (at least in the short run) colour your view. I remember Rupert Murdoch saying to me once, 'You mustn't let these guys [by which he meant the *Guardian*, or *Private Eye* or whoever was attacking me and the *Sunday Times*] edit the newspaper, don't take them into account, you are the editor of the newspaper; you do what you think is right.'

But is it sometimes very difficult to keep to that particular track when there is an overwhelming and persistent weight of criticism coming your way? How do you differentiate the malicious and the ill-informed from criticism which may have some justification?

You have to assume that about 90 per cent of it is malicious and ill-informed, but you also have to trust certain other people's judgements. When you're in a position of power and influence, you are responsible for running the show and an editor of a newspaper has almost dictatorial powers, in a way that a manager or chief executive doesn't necessarily have.

You can't run a newspaper by democracy or by committee, you have got to get the paper out, so you have got to have confidence in your own judgement. But you've also got to be willing to listen and you have got to decide which opinions you will trust and which views you will take into account, even when they are not palatable. You need to build a body of people around you whose judgement you trust. You will not always follow their advice, but you take it into account because you believe it's given with the best of motives.

You have to run a tight ship and make sure that when you decide something, it happens, because you have to carry the can for it, but you also need to create an environment in which there is no penalty for dissent, otherwise you just intimidate people and people will only tell you what you want to hear. You see that with politicians and a lot of chief executives in business.

You cannot afford, particularly if you're in a creative venture, to be surrounded just by 'yes' men, you have got to take the rough with the smooth and you mustn't take it out on people because they tell you things that you don't really want to hear.

And what if the guy who's telling you that you're wrong, who's giving you advice that you trust, wants your job?

I have always taken the view that the more people who wanted my job the better. But this can be a problem for some people – they find it hard to live with a team of very talented people.

The world is too tough and too competitive now, and the other people you are up against are too smart for you not to hire the best and the brightest, and at some stage some of these people should get your job. You should never overstay your welcome, you should move on and do something else. People don't have a lifetime contract on the same job anymore and I have always relished the fact that there were three or four people in my team who could do my job and were probably after it as well. You've also got to let these people have their share of the limelight and take some of the credit. If someone in your team gets the credit for something, by reflection, you get the credit as well. I learned more than anything else – and it took me a while to do so – that the team is all-important; a really strong team which is not afraid to disagree with you, full of people who want your job and one day will get it.

That's healthy; they might start to plot against you if they think you are going to be there forever, and although you may be able to see these plots off, there is nothing more destabilizing or debilitating than office politics.

You talked about the need to move on in pursuing success and the need for the team to know that you are at some stage moving on. Are you saying that success depends on always having another target to move on to, some other area of achievement?

If you are involved in a creative endeavour, it's important not to outstay your welcome. Creativity needs to be constantly replenished and there comes a time when you get settled in your ways and it stops being a challenge. You think, 'Oh well, I've done this before, and I know how to do it.' But it's always better if a fresh mind comes to it.

Everything moves on; we don't operate in an environment anymore where you can be sure who your competitors will be tomorrow. We now live in an age in which you can buy your groceries at the petrol station and you can buy petrol at the supermarket, and in which an airline can start up an insurance company, in which insurance companies can become banks.

So unlike the old days when each industry was well segmented and you knew who all your competitors were, you don't know who is going to start up against you tomorrow and that puts a premium on originality, on being aware of new threats, on always being on the ball, on being excited by what you're doing, on being a total enthusiast. That benefits from changing jobs quite regularly and we now live in a kind of an environment where people will move on. Longevity has its place, but I don't think that in the Information Age it will have the same premium as it did in the Industrial Age where you learned a skill and, although you might have got promoted through the company, that skill stayed with you for life.

Now we constantly need to recharge our batteries and our creative processes, and if you want bright people to work for you, you've got to let them know that they can move up and that you're going to move on. Most newspapers that have run into trouble have really done so because the editor has outstayed his welcome, the owners should have brought someone else to inject some new creativity. Businesses go in waves. The 1960s had a particular *zeitgeist* about them, so did the 1980s, but the 1990s are different and you need people who reflect the mood of the times to be successful in a creative business.

And are we entering an era where people will be successful in four, five, six, seven different ways, perhaps in different careers in the course of their lifetime?

Before one might have gone to university, then become a graduate trainee at the BBC or IBM or wherever, and essentially for the rest of your life you were in that company, but I think the pace of technological change is such that that isn't going to happen any more.

Change used to come in major waves and between them were periods of quiet. We now live in an age of constant waves. In the old industrial days, if you happened to take over at the peak of one wave you could survive ten, 20, 30 years to the next.

I remember my father being made redundant from the Territorial Army in the late 1960s after he had been with them since the end of the war in 1945. He had been in a period of quiet, and then there was a huge upheaval. Nowadays companies are constantly lapped by wave after wave and I think that puts a premium on agility, on creativity, on adaptability and when you take all these things together it also puts a premium on a regular change of personnel, the best and the brightest taking on more than one challenge, not settling for one company for the rest of their lives.

Everything is converging. If you look at the fastest growing industries today and the biggest, most dynamic ones, such as publishing, telecommunications, entertainment, the satellite business, the television business, electronics – all these industries are converging into one seamless whole, you don't know where one ends and where one begins. That convergence process facilitates such people as Barry Diller in the United States who ran the Twentieth Century Fox motion picture studio, then went on to run a shopping channel which acutally made him more money than the movie business; that adaptability will be at a premium and those who have it will survive best of all.

What advice would you give to those people who have grown up in a world where there really has been a kind of progression, a ladder towards success? What you are now saying is that success can come in all kinds of different ways. You might be successful in one particular field, then you might have a fallow period, then go on to be successful at something; maybe you'll be successful early on in your career and not later, which goes against some of the conceptions that people have about gradually rising towards a peak at maybe the age of 50 or 60 where they are really successful. What do you say to people to persuade them to go along with this new and, as you would put it, inevitable concept of success?

They have to realize that nothing is forever, and that if they pursue one single goal and one single ladder of achievement they will never be successful in the exciting businesses of the future. If you do concentrate on doing just one thing all the time and doing that well, you will constantly be overtaken by newcomers coming in and doing it better or doing it differently, or by the changing structure of the market place.

The days of people peaking in their 50s and 60s are gone. I think people will now peak earlier and might then go into a trough which will be difficult for them. If they think, 'I'm only 40 and my best days are over,' they will need a strong psychology to realize it needn't be over; they might have a quiet period and then move on to something else. Adaptability will count for a lot.

There was a certain security in the old system: provided you played the game, and were dedicated to being a company man or woman, you could eventually, with a bit of luck, make it as high as you could go. Security and predictability were what the Industrial Age was all about. We don't live in that age anymore and we must now take the rough with the smooth. A career will be much more like going on a diet now – you sometimes lose weight then put it on, then back down again.

Which means, of course, a different kind of balancing act with your finances?

Yes it does. It means that you cannot count on incomes always growing in real terms and so you have to be careful that when money is coming in, you don't squander it. It will put a premium on individual financial planning to make sure that your lifestyle doesn't suffer during the quieter periods and that you don't have financial worries at a time when you need to be thinking what to do next – getting educated in the latest information technology, for example.

So financial planning in these circumstances becomes a lot more sophisticated; and, another feature of the Information Age, it becomes much more tailored to individuals. It used to be that when you joined a company there was effectively one pension scheme for everybody. By contrast we are going to move much more into individually tailored financial packages, what they call in Silicone Valley 'a cafeteria of compensations', from which you choose the things that most suit your individual needs.

But it is quite difficult for everyone to have a cafeteria of compensations available to them. I wonder whether in the process of this dramatic change that is already upon us, that we've been talking about, whether there are going to be an awful lot of people falling by the wayside and what politicians can do, what governments can do to stop that happening and stop the growth of a huge, disaffected underclass.

A major problem in the Information Age is that society will become a bell-curve. There will be 10 per cent at the bottom who lack the cognitive skills essential in an Information Age, who will have trouble speaking the two languages you have to speak – English and computer. Then there will be a vast majority of people in the middle, who live better lives than they did during the Industrial Age. More will work for themselves and there won't be as many working under terrible conditions, doing tedious jobs on assembly lines. The office girl today, for example, has far better working conditions than the kitchen maid 50 years ago. The same will apply to 80 per cent of society.

Then there will be the final 10 per cent at the top who will be very rich, the Bill Gateses, the Rupert Murdochs, the people who really do well out of the Information Age.

The real problem lies with that 10 per cent at the bottom. Nobody quite knows what to do about them, especially if that 10 per cent mirrors the evidence now beginning to come through from America. They are not there because they are disadvantaged, because they are discriminated against, or because they never got a start in life; they are there because they lack the basic cognitive skills to prosper in this kind of society. They are the consequence of the meritocracy, the ones that fall through the net and it is among them that most of the social problems arise. They become an underclass.

When I first brought the phrase 'underclass' to Britian in the late 1980s, Mrs Thatcher said there was no such thing in Britain, and the left said that the underclass was just another name for the poor working class. The underclass is not a degree of poverty, some underclass people actually have more disposable income than ordinary working-class folk.

The underclass is a type of poverty which takes you out of the norms of society altogether. Working-class people in the 1930s had the same aspirations and norms and values as middle-class people, they just didn't have the same amount of money and the same amount of opportunity. This underclass is in a different category altogether and what happens to these people is one of the problems of an Information Age.

Do people who are successful have an obligation to the underclass?

Yes, I think they do. They have a moral obligation to try to do something about it and I think they have a self-interest to do something about it as well, otherwise they are going to end up living in gated communities, as they call them in America, and these underclasses will be herded into reservations, in effect, which we now call ghettos or sink estates, from where the crime will break out and from where the fear in the rest of society will come. So for both moral reasons and for reasons of self-preservation, more and more effort will need to go into helping that underclass, and we should be able to do it because the Information Age is producing people who are not just rich, they are mega-rich.

Some individuals in computing and the media are worth up to 18 billion dollars, more than the GNP of a small country in Latin America; so I think, 'What can you do with 18 billion dollars?' I am moderately well off already and I am not desperate for that much more money, and I think that the mega-rich should use their surfeit of money to get involved and sort out the problems of the underclass.

You came not from a poor background, but an ordinary one in Paisley. To what extent has your success now been based on your background and upbringing?

I think that it's a necessary element in the success that I've enjoyed. There is something within you that makes you motivated and want to get on anyway; you either have that or you can develop it, regardless of background. But I was lucky to have a number of essential building blocks which gave me a solid base.

Firstly, there was a good family life with *two* parents; the value of which we are only now coming to appreciate, regardless of the background that you are from.

Secondly, I was fortunate to have one of the best educations that you can have and one that many people in England would have had to pay a great deal to get. I had a very good school and a very good university.

Thirdly, I had a strong moral base with the influence of the Church of Scotland and Presbyterianism. I think I benefited very much from the combination of family, the Church of Scotland (which helped to give you a moral compass and also reinforce that sense that you can help yourself) and an education system which was essentially open to talented people regardless of background and gave them a world-class education as a result. These three reinforced each other – the family, the church, the school – in producing a feeling that if you wanted to get on in life, you got yourself a decent education and you worked hard.

There was nothing you couldn't achieve even if, initially, you were held back because you didn't come from the right background. There were so many examples of people who 'didn't come from the right background' who got on that it didn't matter that others might try to stop you – you knew you could get on.

So where did your desire for success and achievement come from?

I think it was a combination of that cultural background and something genetic, because there are plenty of other people from my background who had a similar home life and similar education and opportunities, but who have not progressed as far in their chosen career.

When was the first time that you said to yourself, 'I have been successful,' or, 'Wow, I can be a success at something, I can achieve something'?

Because the school I went to was so success-orientated, or at least academic-orientated, I often felt that things were going well in that I was doing well in exams. The competition was tough, there were a lot of other bright kids in the school and I was never first, but I was up there with the leaders and I felt, 'If I carry on like this, things are going to work out well.' Every time you feel that, of course, the next challenge arrives.

When I went from my local primary school in the middle of the council estate to the grammar school in the centre of town, that was a huge challenge. I felt I had been successful at the primary school, but then, instead of being the big fish in a small pond, I became a small fish in the big pond. In the six years that I was there, all seemed to click into place then came university, which is another huge challenge and you think, 'Is this going to work?' It did.

Next came the world of work and, again, every time you think you are being a success another challenge comes along. When Alistair Burnett gave me my first major job at *The Economist* in 1973, I felt that that was another huge challenge, because although I had had a successful track record behind me at school and university, each level of success or challenge widened the net of competition. Now I was moving from Glasgow University into a magazine that was largely dominated by some of the best and the brightest from Oxford and Cambridge, so there was a doubt in my mind: I've done pretty well so far but am I up to being in their league? Then you find that you are, and when I moved from *The Economist* to the *Sunday Times* I remember in that transition period being very worried, too. I had done *The Economist* for ten years; that had turned out to be a success and some Oxbridge firsts turned out to be not as bright as they thought they were. But the *Sunday Times* was a world-famous newspaper and I had never even worked in a newspaper. I think that it's important, as you become successful and take on a new challenge, not to assume that you are necessarily going to be a success. Doubts about your ability to do something are healthy.

How great were those doubts, (a) when you were asked to go to The Economist *and (b) when you were asked to go to the* Sunday Times?

The doubts were greater when I went to the *Sunday Times*. Because I was much younger – I was only 24 – when I joined *The Economist,* I had the arrogance and enthusiasm of youth. It seemed a natural progression to go to somewhere like *The Economist.*

I had done a degree in politics and economics, I had worked in the Conservative Research Department and for 18 months with Peter Walker at the Environment Department.

For a 24-year-old I was relatively well informed about the ways of Westminster and about some of the big issues of the day, and I felt that although I was moving into a far tougher environment, I would probably be OK.

The jump from *The Economist* to the *Sunday Times* was huge and it caused me a lot more worries because it was moving into an area that I didn't know much about. As the *Guardian* pointed out about three times when the announcement was made, I had never even worked on a national newspaper before, never mind edited one. I knew I was moving into a hostile environment as well. They didn't like this new guy coming in from the outside, and I didn't know how I was going to be able to handle Murdoch as a proprietor either. I had a great fear that I would be caught in a vice between a demanding proprietor on the one hand and a surly staff on the other.

So given all these doubts, why take the job?

Because the challenge was so great, though I had my one and only anxiety attack flying from Denver to New York in that transition period. I got a nervous churning in my stomach: I couldn't quite work out what it was, but clearly, in retrospect, it was the subconscious worry of the job looming a month ahead at the *Sunday Times*. Although it did worry me and I was very apprehensive that when I went there it was just going to be a disaster, nevertheless when someone offers you, at the age of 34, the chance to edit one of the world's most famous newspapers, you have to take it.

Are there any other areas of your life, or indeed any other areas of your profession, that you regard as failures?

I think my people-management skills were not a great success. Dealing with creative people, I found it very hard to indulge them and to have time for their egos, and I tended to be too slow to praise success and too quick and too harsh to criticize failure. Although too much ego-massaging goes on, you do need to do some of it, people do feel the need to be appreciated. And if they have done something badly or wrongly, you can be too brutal in telling them that. People are all fragile to some extent and I think I was sometimes too ruthless.

It partly came out of the period when I first went to the paper and knew everybody was against me. The atmosphere was pretty brutal to begin with, and I felt that if I wasn't as ruthless as they were, I would lose. The problem was, that as I began to win and build a team more in my shape and more to my liking, I didn't soften the edges quickly enough. Of course, the whole dispute over the move to Wapping and the new practices set us back again as well, that soured relationships with the staff again and made for a very difficult time. But by 1990–91 I had been in the job about seven or eight years, and I should have loosened up and lightened up earlier than I did.

I think even the people at the *Sunday Times* would admit that by 1992, '93 or '94 the change in my demeanour had resulted in a change in the whole atmosphere at the paper, in that it was a happier, friendlier place at which to work.

If I were doing it again, or in a similar position, I would be keener to inspire and help rather than criticize all the time. That's not to say that some people don't need a bollocking every now and then – we all do – but I overdid it.

Do you have any particular formula for gearing yourself up to deal with the slings and arrows of outrageous fortune?

I think the single biggest thing which harks back to my education and background, is that if you are going to get into a fight and a lot of powerful forces are going to be ranged against you, the first fundamental thing you have to do is do your homework. You've got to know your subject, you've got to have confidence that what you believe or what you are doing is right, and you have got to have covered all the angles – you have got to become a master of that subject. That's what makes a good journalist.

A good journalist is someone who might not be an expert in something, but can pick up the fundamentals of almost anything very quickly and is then smart enough, having learned these fundamentals, to take on the arguments. I remember Alistair Burnett saying to me once, when I was attacked over something I had done, that my oppponents were attacking me personally because they had lost the argument. He said although that can be painful or hurtful, it's actually a victory; and there's some sense in that.

You've mentioned Alistair Burnett a couple of times. Are you more likely to be successful if you have a mentor, someone who, at the right time of your life, decides that you are worth backing and supporting?

I think it does help. Sometimes it can be your father, but in my case it couldn't, because although my father was a lovely man and I loved him, he was a gentle, unambitious man, a simple man in the nice sense of the word. He'd left school at 15, he didn't have a university education and he knew nothing about journalism, so he couldn't be my mentor given the area that I was going to go into.

I was fortunate to meet someone like Alistair Burnett who was doing what I wanted to do (which was to be a print journalist and a broadcaster) who spoke with great authority on many subjects, who took time to encourage talent, who had a great sense of humour and who had certain standards about writing and journalism that I thought were worth following. I always remember when I got something wrong in an article and he gave me – as only Alistair could do – a gentle bollocking, he was too gentle a man to make it too harsh. I said, 'But it's a scoop, Alistair, I just got that one little thing wrong.' But he said, 'Yes, but if you can't get the small things right, how can we trust you for the big things?' Things like that; and the fact that he would take the time to care.

In the middle of the Wapping problems, when I had two bodyguards with me almost everywhere I went and received lots of death threats, when the whole of the British establishment was essentially against what we were trying to do, I would get home at about ten o'clock and I would watch him on *News At Ten* and the phone would ring at about 10.30 almost within 30 seconds of his being off air, and he would say, 'I thought if you were at home I would come round and take a drink off you,' and he would come over and stay until one in the morning.

The fact that someone who had given me my first major job was still, 10 years later, prepared to come round and just lend his support, really mattered to me. I have tried to do the same with some of the younger journalists I have worked with because I know how important Alistair was to me.

When you went to America, you left the Sunday Times, *albeit at the time apparently temporarily, in order to go for what you clearly perceived to be your big break in television journalism. It didn't work out. Were you really taken aback by that and how did you pick yourself up after Murdoch had said, 'Look we are not going to run with this programme,' how did you then say, 'I've got to pick myself up, enter the fray again and try to re-establish my success'?*

I didn't perceive it as my big break in television, I would have been amazed if it had worked. What I did perceive was a lucrative move away from the *Sunday Times*, which is what it was. I had been with the paper for over ten years by then. I was getting restless and didn't want to outstay my welcome; what's more Rupert Murdoch was getting restless at having a too independent-minded editor, too much of a celebrity.

That was one of the things that used to annoy him more than anything else, whereas I rather relished the celebrity status or even the notoriety, it was one of the reasons for being at the *Sunday Times*.

Were there any times when you felt like giving it all up?

There were a couple of times, and I suppose that's when the quality of the people around you is most important, because they can help to lift your spirits again and rally round you. In the immediate aftermath of the move to Wapping, when most of the staff had turned against me and the move and it was such a brutal fight, I felt I was fighting a battle without an army or at least with a most reluctant army. But then Murdoch stepped in and made it clear that if the staff wanted to take me on then they would take him on as well, and that made them step back.

Were you tempted to resign at that point?

Well, I just felt that I was losing it and that the confidence of the staff had gone. They were miserable. I felt I had almost no support in the paper and that I was in a very difficult position. I am not sure that, at the end of the day, if they had gone ahead with their motion of no confidence, even if they had voted that way, I would not have bashed on without them because I was so committed to the fight. But it was certainly a low point; I did think that I might have to resign and throw it all in.

There was another time when I came very close to it and I think I would have had to resign if the events had gone the way that I feared. This was in the libel trial against Peregrine Worsthorne who had written an editorial saying that I was unfit to be editor of the *Sunday Times* because of the Pamela Bordes episode: she had briefly been a girlfriend of mine in the summer of 1988, and then about six months later it had been revealed that she had been a highly-paid call girl. I had fought the libel case on the basis that since I was single and she was single, I could only be unfit to be editor if I had known that she was a call girl; and I had not. It was unfortunate, it was embarrassing, it was unlucky, but I didn't see why it made me unfit, and I fought this libel case to establish my integrity and good name and also take on a man whom I regarded as a pompous windbag for writing all this.

In retrospect it was a mistake, because the consequences of failure were not worth the risk of success. His piece had annoyed me and hurt me. It had been a serious attack and there was always the risk of the allegation being brought up again in the future. If I had lost, the financial cost would have been huge and all my enemies would have had a field day, which would probably have made it impossible for me to carry on as editor.

On the upside, if we beat them, we beat them and that was the end of it. It was a lottery – I won in the end, but I just won and no more, and it could easily have gone the other way.

And you did actually consider what might happen if the verdict went against you?

I remember the jury went out in the morning at about 11 o'clock and I had a deadening feeling in the pit of my stomach about the consequences of defeat. I went to the RAC Club and I just sat there on my own in a side room sipping mineral water. I couldn't eat anything, I could barely swallow the water. I didn't want to be with anyone. Through the trial I'd always lunched with some of my other editors because I was still editing the paper and I needed all the time I could find, but that day I didn't want to be with anybody at all. My driver dropped me off at the RAC and I sat there until about 2.30 and contemplated the consequences of defeat. It would be the end of my career as a newspaper editor and I would have huge legal bills to pick up as well. I would probably have had to sell the house or re-mortgage it, and, frankly, just to put Peregrine Worsthorne in his place, it wasn't worth it, it was too big a risk. To have risked all that was a big mistake.

Out of this, have you developed any ground rules for any advice you would give to people for dealing with an unexpected moment when everything you have worked for seems suddenly and dramatically threatened?

The first thing is to try to avoid getting into a situation like that by not taking decisions in anger. I reacted too viscerally to too many things. Sometimes in a creative business that's quite useful – if your gut instincts are right, that's helpful. But at other times you'd be better, metaphorically, to go and lie down in a dark room on your own for a while, then come to a decision.

If you write a letter in anger, don't post it that night, wait and read it again in the morning before you send it, because you might take a different view. I would often dash off memos to people because they had done something that really annoyed me and later on I would regret that I had been so hostile. If it is something that really threatens you, take longer to make the decision. You don't have to react right away.

You've been the reporter, you've been the reported, is there something intrinsically unfair or not about the way in which people who achieve a degree of success in their lives become targets?

There is an element in our society which despises success. Successful people all over the world are targets and that's part of the price of success; and it might actually be quite a good controlling mechanism.

There is what's called the 'tall poppy syndrome' and even in America, such a success-orientated country, you still see a degree of envy. But this is the only country in the world, or the only advanced country, in which it seems to be a crime to try too hard and where ambition is regarded as a flaw. There is still an element in our culture which implies that everything should happen with effortless ease and that you shouldn't try too hard, you shouldn't compete, it should all just fall into your lap through the grace of being a gentleman and being in the right place at the right time.

When you don't behave like that and are more competitive and take risks, there is a segment in the 'chattering-class' society that rather resents it and they gang up on you. It's interesting that even in left-wing novels, the hero is always the person who inherited things rather than the self-made person.

Susan Crosland was married to a Labour minister years ago and is still part of the centre-left chattering class; she is a charming woman, but in her first novel the hero was the inheriting Alec Douglas-Home type of Tory and the villain was the self-made Margaret Thatcher kind of Tory.

In your enthusiasm for self-made success, is there no room at all for inherited success, do you think that people who have inherited large fortunes are, in a sense, not tested or tried or proved by the world at large?

No, I think that a lot of inherited wealth is now tested. If you take someone like Vere Rothermere who essentially inherited the *Daily Mail.* If he had been no use, the *Daily Mail* wouldn't have survived today, because it operates in the most competitive newspaper market in the world, but he's taken something he's inherited and made an even bigger success of it.

I think there is room for inherited wealth provided that that wealth isn't squandered. If on the other hand the Earl of

Cadogan simply inherits prime property in Chelsea and just sits on it then there's no great future in that, that's not adding any jobs, that's not adding to the wealth of the country. Vere Rothermere has made a contribution, he's created jobs and profits and paid his taxes. People who inherit have a duty to make something of it and to build on it, whereas so often it just atrophies.

I am also concerned about the proportions in which tax is paid. We all have to pay tax, but how come that so often we pay more tax on income that we work hard for than that got through the accident of inheritence. It would seem to me, in a society that wants to be meritocratic and socially mobile, that we should tax less those who work hardest for their money, at any income level – because there are plenty of people working hard in this country for not much money, who are still paying a lot of tax on that money – while those who get their money through the accident of birth should pay a bit more.

Do you make your own luck on the path to success?

You do make a lot of your own luck, but you have to have lucky breaks as well. When I got my degree in 1971, I didn't know what I was going to do and I thought like many others, 'If you don't know what to do, then do another degree.' But I also stood for election as chairman of the Federation of Conservative Students and I won; that was quite lucky because that gave me a job in the Conservative Research Department and propelled me straight from university into the heart of Westminster.

Otherwise we may not have seen Andrew Neil, journalist?

I think that's right and also I was lucky that Alistair Burnett was editor of *The Economist* when I applied for a job because up to then it had tended to recruit almost exclusively from just a few specific colleges at Oxford and Cambridge. The fact that Alistair had come from Scotland and still had a house in Glasgow, where I had gone to university, was very lucky. A more English-establishment character might not have even given me an interview. So that was lucky as well.

I also think that if Lord Thomson had still owned *The Times*, I would never have made the move to the *Sunday Times*. It took someone like Rupert Murdoch to take the risk of appointing an unknown 34-year-old to be its editor, so although you can make your own luck in the sense that you can position yourself to take advantage of opportunities, I was also very lucky someone like Murdoch owned the paper at that time. The cards have to fall the right way

Who are your heroes. Who are the people you regard, past or present, as being people who you look up to, as being the ultimate perhaps in success?

Well, although she and I never got on all that well together, I must say as time goes on, Margaret Thatcher has become a bit of a hero. I suppose we live in an age of political pygmies now, and she begins to look more and more like a giant. Although she often used to infuriate me, I think basically what she stood for was right and this country is a much better place for it.

John MacIntosh, the Labour MP, was also one of my heroes, he was an academic and he was a social democrat ahead of his time. He and I were about to write a book together when he died far too young.

Thomas Jefferson is my hero among American Presidents, because he combined great statesmanship with a huge intellectual grasp of the issues. He was the philosopher king in many ways, and also had a view of the devolution of power. He was the one that coined the phrase, 'The best government is least government'. He also wrote that his two biggest intellectual influences were really the biggest influences on the American Revolution. They were Adam Smith who wrote *The Wealth of Nations* at the University of Glasgow, and David Hume, who was the leading philosopher at Edinburgh University at the time – the Scottish Enlightenment and my own university tradition. If your mentor can be your hero, I would also put Alistair Burnett up there as one of my heroes.

What do you think are the greatest enemies of success?

The main enemy of success is a conservatism that takes the view that it's always been done this way, that there is no conceivable better way of doing it, and even if there is we don't want to know about it, because we are comfortable doing it this way.

I think that's the kind of attitude that took hold in Britain (and looked like it was going to take hold of America as well in the 1970s, but didn't) that made us think that we built the best ships in the world, the best cars in the world, the best machine tools and so on, when we were still making them the way we had done in Victorian times and the rest of the world had moved on and started to make them better and more efficiently. I now worry every time I hear someone saying we have the best broadcasting in the world, that it's going to go the way British Leyland did. That is the real enemy of success: an inability to conceive of other better ways of doing something. It applies whether you are running a company or running a country.

What is your greatest pleasure from the fruits of your success?

I think the greatest pleasure now is being my own independent self: being happy with myself and satisfied, feeling independent and feeling that I am now in control of events; that I call the shots and have financial security.

The thing about money and financial security is the freedom and independence it gives you. It's not collecting valuable things, it's the security of knowing that you are not dependent on anybody else and that you don't have to worry about where the next pay cheque is coming from.

If you could gather before you in one room all the budding young journalists in the world who had their feet poised on the first step of the ladder of their career, what advice would you give to them for them to become as successful in their journalistic career as you have been?

I would advise them to have one foot in print and one in broadcasting, to master the skills of both. I would advise them not to go to an American school of journalism; that would take away all the creativity they ever had. I would advise that if they haven't got an inquiring mind then they shouldn't be in journalism, because what makes a great journalist above all is that spirit of inquiry, being interested in things and being enthusiastic about something. If they haven't got that they they shouldn't go into it because all they will end up doing is writing diaries sneering about people or compiling frothy feature columns. If they want to be real journalists they should be inquisitive, they should feel passionately about things and they should, in this age, be multi-skilled – able to write and edit tape and broadcast.

When your time comes to leave this planet, what would you like people to say about you?

I think: 'He was his own man; we might not have agreed with him, but he believed in what he did and he wasn't in anybody's pocket. He cared for his country and for those around him.'

FRANÇOIS PIENAAR

Few who witnessed the historic television pictures will easily forget the moving moment in June 1995 when sport cemented and enhanced the new post-apartheid South Africa. Their team, the Springboks, had just defied the pundits to win rugby's World Cup in front of an ecstatic home crowd of black and white faces. François Pienaar, their captain, watched in astonishment as his country's President, Nelson Mandela, walked across the pitch wearing what had been seen as a symbol of white supremacy – a Springbok jersey.

Unquestionably his country's most influential sportsman, he had for years been quietly coaching disadvantaged youngsters from the black townships.

Four words shape his attitude to both sport and life – discipline, dedication, desire and determination. He believes that you have to experience failure to grow, and describes here how he overcame a strong urge to quit the national side; and how a tour of New Zealand, widely seen in South Africa as a disaster, actually paved the way for the World Cup success.

He now avoids reading those parts of newspapers where he or his team are mentioned, preferring 'the constructive criticism of his coach to the negative criticism of the media'. He reveals the technique for restoring team spirit when they thought they'd lost the World Cup: 'we addressed the worst fears of each member of the team – both as a player and as a human being.'

He believes his passionate advocacy of professionalism in rugby later cost him his place in the Springbok team. Now in London playing for the ambitious club, Saracens, he still harbours hopes of reclaiming his place on the national side. This interview with the man once labelled 'the most destructive loose forward in rugby' probes his approach to winning the World Cup, and his views on both personal and team success. He also reveals an encouraging, catalytic moment at the tender age of eight when 'I felt like I was the best thing that ever touched a rugby ball'.

François Pienaar, what is your definition of success?

A successful person is a person that's consistently good at something. It's no use being good at something only once. You've got to be consistently good at something. Only then are you truly professional or truly successful.

Are you more successful if you've experienced failure?

You have to experience failure to grow; you have to experience it to become bigger. A wise person is not only someone who learns from another's mistakes; he definitely learns from his own.

Are there any things you regard as particular failures which you built upon to create success?

Yes, I've experienced failure: I've experienced highs and lows in my rugby, on both a provincial level and an international level. As a team I think our toughest assignment – though I wouldn't call it unsuccessful, in fact I thought it was one of our successful tours – was in New Zealand in 1994; everybody rated it as one of the worst tours ever, but if you looked afterwards at the percentage of games we won, we actually came out as one of the top touring sides.

Because we didn't win a Test match people saw the whole tour as a failure; but we went to New Zealand without any experience whatsoever of their conditions, of playing together as a team, of their refereeing, of playing in New Zealand in front of their crowds. In fact when we played in Wellington, the wind blew so hard in front of the poles that our full-back couldn't even kick it over from the 22-metre line – that never happens in South Africa. Personally I saw that tour as a valuable learning experience, but a lot of people in South Africa saw it as a disaster; and when the team came back, many changes were made to the coaches, management and so on.

The following year, in the World Cup, we played against France in Durban in some of the worst conditions I've ever seen in South Africa, but we weren't worried about the weather because we'd experienced New Zealand; if we hadn't had that tour, we wouldn't have been so successful in the World Cup. We had learned from that less successful tour and so, when we went on to the field at Durban, nobody spoke about the weather, just about beating France.

You've had criticism in your time. How do you cope with that?

I'll have criticism in the future as well; I'll always have criticism. It's a simple thing that you can't please all the people all the time and that's what I live by. You can only please some of the people some of the time, especially in South Africa – they are very provincial-minded I've always had the wind from the front, always, and I'll still have it. I don't know why, I can't say why. If I look back at my career, I cope with criticism by my awareness that I've really broken all the records that I can break in South Africa, and that is enough for me.

Did you ever feel like giving up?

Never. I just felt like redirecting my energies. At one stage I felt like retiring from the Springbok team and just playing provincial rugby because of the demands and the pressures, but as the saying goes, 'If you can't stand the heat get out of the kitchen.' In life one can always see the negatives; in fact many people don't like to look at the positives, but I started looking at the positives; I changed my attitude and looked at the positive things that have come out of rugby, not the negative things. I don't read sections of newspapers dealing with rugby since many articles about me are written by those who, quite frankly, I don't respect as people who know the game. So when I read newspapers I avoid the section where I myself, or the team, might be mentioned.

Does that apply to the rest of the team as well?

No. A lot of the players, especially the younger guys, read newspapers because at that age you like to hear about yourself and read about yourself, but I try and get them away from it. The only way you can keep on track and keep growing as a player is to work on the positives of your game. The criticism will come, from the coach and from the other players, but it will be constructive criticism. Not the negative criticism that comes from those outside the game.

What do you reckon were the most successful moments of your life? Not on the sporting field, but those that perhaps we don't know about, that aren't on public record, when you've said to yourself, 'This has been a great triumph for me, this has been an enormous success.' I'll give you an example: when I was talking to the British Prime Minister, he said that he really thought he'd been successful for the first time when his salary passed the £2,000-a-year mark. Do you have any equivalent of that, not necessarily financial, but in any area of achievement?

Yes. When we went to New Zealand, the team was in really bad shape. We had no confidence. As I said, we were criticised severely in South Africa – we were actually in hiding the night before the first Test. But the way we planned, and I worked with the team throughout that tour, was a personal triumph – we eventually came away with a draw in the third Test and actually we should have beaten them – they were lucky to get the draw. When I came back I just felt so ecstatic about the way we'd developed. As a team captain and as a team player I felt I'd accomplished a great deal with the players.

And anything in your personal life, your early life perhaps. What was your first success? When did you first feel, 'I've been successful, I am successful'?

Well, when I was eight years old, I played No.8. My Dad and my uncle came to watch me and they promised me a rand for every try that I scored, and a rand in those days was a hell of lot of money. I scored eight tries for my team and I felt like I was the best thing that ever touched a rugby ball. That is the fondest memory I have from my childhood.

Do you need total control to obtain success? Have you got to be in charge, ruthlessly driving everything through or do you rely on others for success?

You have to rely on others because you don't have the vision yourself. That's why I said earlier that you have to learn from your mistakes and you have to learn from others. You don't live in the past but it's a fool who doesn't look back at his past and especially in a team game like ours. I listen to advice every day and I take advice because you get into a rut, you really do; you start believing that everything you say is the best, you never assume that you are wrong and don't judge yourself anymore, yet you need to judge yourself and you get the best judgement of your character when you listen to others.

Which is more difficult – team success or individual success?

They are different types of success. Individual success in a team game is easier than team success because you can play for yourself and be the best player on the park, but your game will be selfish. You may be regarded as a fantastic player, but the vision to play a central role in a successful team, to put the team in front of your personal aspirations – that is more difficult to achieve.

Is there a difference in the way that you plan success or the way that you achieve? You might, for example, sit down with your team and plan the way you want a game to develop, then the unexpected comes up, in a way that you haven't thought about, and you've got to react instinctively to that, to reclaim the success that you were trying to achieve.

No, you always plan for the unexpected as well. You have Plan B as well as Plan A. That's what we did in the World Cup. We planned to win the World Cup. We didn't just go out and say, 'If we win this World Cup it will be fantastic, if we win the cup it will be great,' we planned it and took it step by step. But we also planned for disaster, and for what would happen after disaster. The World Cup was in South Africa and South Africa is fierce when it comes to rugby, so if we lost the first game – which everybody thought we were going to do – what would we do after that? Would we just lie down or would we come back a better team and work from there? Your Plan B must also be a serious plan of action.

Was there any stage in the World Cup when you really felt that things were not going to plan and that you were in real danger of losing out?

Yes. When two of our players were suspended after the Canadian game. This was unfair and I still maintain that they were not treated in the right way. Video material shows that we just tried to play the game, whereas Canada came out and provoked us; they had everything to gain and nothing to lose. After that game our team spirit was very low, but we continued to train with the same commitment – though to be honest I felt we were going to lose the World Cup right there and then.

So how did you pick yourself up and recover from that?

We said before the World Cup that if something like that happened, we would need to sit down and discuss it, and we did. New players came into the side, and I used the new players to help pick up the team spirit. Chester Williams had missed out on the initial World Cup squad through injury and now, all of a sudden, he was back in the side; and his delight at being back in the side, I think, lifted the team. We had to get the team spirit back, because team spirit made the team. On paper we might not have had the best team of individuals, but we did have the best team as a unit and had the team spirit been lost we would not have been successful. That was the thing that we had to work on. First of all, in dealing with this problem, we addressed the worst fears of each member of the team both as a player and as a human being. When these fears are in the open and everyone knows about them, they don't seem not so much of a problem anymore; 90 per cent of things that you worry about never actually happen.

There is a saying that you make your own luck. Do you believe that?

Yes, I do. This year, when we were in a bad patch, we were not successful – basically because we had lost the principles that we believed in – and people said we were unlucky. But it's not a lack of luck that makes you lose, it's the letting go of the principles by which you play, that loses your luck in sport.

Is luck an essential part of success?

You need breaks, but I think you make your own breaks.

Is there a difference, do you think, between sporting success and success in other fields, such as business and politics, or are there core similarities that run right through?

No, of course there are core similarities that run right through. I believe in the four Ds in life: discipline, dedication, desire and determination. They apply in sport and life in general.

Are there any people, big or small, in any profession, either living now or in history, whom you hugely admire as being at the pinnacle of success as you rate it?

Yes. President De Klerk and President Mandela for making the change in South Africa's government and for not resenting what had happened in the past. I really respect them as leaders. That to me was one of the biggest steps, and it's just a pity that President De Klerk is not getting the acclaim that he deserves because he took a step that could have gone either way.

Anybody outside politics?

I respect my coach tremendously for what he has taught me. He's taught me a hell of a lot of things, but his way of handling situations and handling players is his biggest skill. He doesn't talk about it, but he's had cancer for 16 years; he fights through it and nobody ever knows about it. The success he's achieved as a human being, in his business and in rugby, is phenomenal. And the way he goes about it is an eye-opener. It's easy to get big-headed when you win the World Cup, it's easy to get big-headed when you are a top rugby player – it's the way that you handle it that makes you a better person.

And how does he handle it? How does he go about it?

The way he handled it when he was nothing; when he was just a nobody. The same way. He's down to earth, he's noble, he listens to people and he uses what he learns from people to overcome his weaknesses or to help him.

Is it becoming more or less difficult to achieve success in your particular field?

Much more difficult. What can you achieve after you've won the World Cup? People say when you have reached the top of a mountain there is only one way and that's down. Yes, you must go down, but when you get to the bottom, I believe there will be another bigger mountain to be climbed. It may be in rugby, it may be in life. So success shouldn't be channelled only into one thing. I think quality of life is also very important to me.

Success arouses conflicting emotions in people. Some admire it tremendously, others feel very envious about other people's success. What do you say to those people who feel envy about success?

I don't think it's envy, I think it's jealousy more than envy – certainly what I've experienced in South Africa is more jealousy than envy. Because I believe people who are envious of another person will want to learn, whereas people who are jealous only criticize. Envious people are easy to work with because they listen to advice; jealous people see the wrong in the right. A great many people have been involved in the transition to professionalism in rugby, and there has been a lot of jealousy and suspicion. I was often depicted as the black sheep who was trying to ruin South African rugby, but if you speak to any rugby player or anybody else involved, you'll find that I only spoke my mind; I was always open and honest about it.

So was it a difficult time for you?

The most difficult time of my life, but if I look back I wouldn't have done anything different.

And how did you deal with the jealousy?

I'm still dealing with it, it's just that I listen to people that I respect, people that have given me advice and people that have guided me. You must have an alter ego and I've definitely got one. I've got a very close relationship with a coach and also with a family member who helps me, and I use them constantly to guide me and give me advice.

If you could gather all the young rugby players in the world – youngsters of 12, 14, 16, fanatical rugby fans – in one room and give them one piece of advice about how they could become as successful as you are, what would that be?

Never to stop dreaming. Because my success started with a dream and dreams can come true if you apply your mind. The way to go about it is never to lose your dream. If you lose your dream then you've got nothing to work for.

When your time comes to leave this Earth, what would you like them to say about you?

There's really no one thing I would like said about me. Perhaps just that I gave it my best.

There's nothing you would like to say – 'They must remember me for this,' or, 'I hope they'll remember me…'

There's nothing that I would really like to suggest on the lines of, 'I've done this and that.' No, I would like people to remember me for what I have given them; I hope I've given a lot of people a lot of pleasure. And if they remember me for the right things, it doesn't really matter what it is for because different people will remember different things. Players would remember differently from spectators and administrators, for example.

What would you expect your fellow team members to say?

I hope they would just respect me for all that I stood for, and for the fact that I never compromised the team for myself.